ROME IN THE LATE REPUBLIC

Mary Beard &
Michael Crawford

D0142534

Cornell University Press
Ithaca, New York

First published in 1985 by Cornell University Press

Library of Congress Cataloguing in Publication Data

Beard, Mary.
　Rome in the late Republic.

　Bibliography: p.
　Includes index.
　1. Rome—History—Republic, 265-30 B.C.
I. Crawford, Michael H. (Michael Hewson), 1939-
II. Title
DG254.B37　1985　　　　937'.02　　　　　　85-480
ISBN 0-8014-1824-0

Printed in Great Britain.

Contents

Preface

This book is the result of a happy co-operation—not only between the two authors, who have survived their partnership without a serious quarrel, but also between the authors and many of their friends, who have generously read and commented on all or part of the text. Special thanks are due to Keith Hopkins, who improved not only the argument, but also the English of all he read; and also to Graham Burton, Averil Cameron, Robin Cormack, John Crook (for kind instruction in Roman Law), Carlotta Dionisotti, John North, Simon Price, Richard Saller and Brent Shaw. We have happily incorporated many of their suggestions. They bear no responsibility where we have wilfully ignored them.

We should also like to thank Joyce Reynolds, not for any help with this book—which is a present for her—but for all that she has taught us both over many years.

W.M.B.

M.H.C.

Introduction

Cicero would have disapproved of this book. He would have been distressed to find his own part in it so small; and he probably would not have seen why we have defined the problems of the late Republic in the way we have. That is precisely what we intended. It is impossible now to understand the first century BC in first-century terms. We have aimed at a far more straightforward—and at the same time more challenging—goal: that is to make the first century make sense for us in our own twentieth-century terms.

We have written a short book—again unlike Cicero! For most of our readership—some sixth-formers, undergraduates and their teachers—we imagine that this will seem a considerable advantage. But inevitable consequences follow. First we have had to assume some basic knowledge of the narrative history and physical environment of the late Republic. Absolute beginners are advised to read the relevant sections of Scullard's *Gracchi to Nero* and Brunt's *Social Conflicts* before turning to what we have to say. They are also advised to acquire some grasp of the geography of Italy and the Mediterranean—see, for example, T.J. Cornell and J. Matthews, *Atlas of the Roman World* (Oxford, 1982). Secondly, we have been forced to be highly selective. Most of our own favourite topics are included, and our favourite books and articles mentioned. We apologise in advance to those who find their own favourites missing.

The main text stands on its own; but the footnotes form an important part of the book, in providing a guide to further reading on many topics we have treated sketchily. In writing these footnotes we have decided to refer to no works in languages other than English (except picture books) and to indicate, where possible, the degree of difficulty of the works we do cite. Full details of works cited by short title only may be found in the Bibliography, which also lists all the other modern literature we have mentioned. Since we assume our readers will have become familiar with Brunt's *Social Conflicts* and Scullard's *Gracchi to Nero*, we have not normally mentioned them in our notes; they are relevant to a very large part of what we have to say. The Appendix lists readily available translations of ancient sources we have cited.

Chapter One

THE NATURE OF THE PROBLEM

By the mid-first century BC, the republican form of government at Rome had effectively collapsed. Out of this collapse there emerged, in the aftermath of civil war, first the dictatorship of Caesar and then the principate of Augustus. In a swift and striking transformation, a political system founded upon principles fundamentally opposed to monarchy was replaced by a system monarchical in all but name.

So far, the narrative is simple—and would not be questioned by any historian, ancient or modern.

By contrast, the causes of the collapse and the steps which led up to the final outbreak of civil war are far from straightforward. The modern literature on the subject is vast and there are many areas of controversy. Different occasions have been proposed as the ultimate origin of the revolution. Different events have been accorded special significance in the build up to civil war. Historians have isolated different factors in the search for the underlying cause for the whole process. So, for example, in some accounts (ancient and modern) we find the breaking point set in 133 BC—when political conflict led to violence and the tribune Tiberius Gracchus was lynched. In others it is set in 60 BC—when Pompey, Caesar and Crassus formed an unofficial compact which effectively dominated the operation of politics. This diversity is illuminating; for it throws into prominence many events whose significance might otherwise be overlooked. But it also causes problems, presenting us with a series of seemingly mutually exclusive explanations for the collapse of the Republic.[1]

The idea that there was a single start to the process is itself problematic. Scholars have always recognised that any sharp boundary

---

1. Asinius Pollio (76 BC- AD 4) chose 60 BC as the starting point of his *History of the Civil Wars*; likewise Syme, *Roman Revolution* (see, especially, pp. 1-9). The *Civil Wars* of Appian (written in the second century AD) and Scullard's *Gracchi to Nero* start, by contrast, in 133 BC. For other views on the 'turning point' of late Republican history, see Gruen, *Last Generation*, esp. 1-5 and 498-507 (but note the criticisms of M.H.Crawford, *JRS* 66 (1976), 214-217); and Badian, 'Gracchi to Sulla', 215.

between one period and another is necessarily artificial; but they have still had to choose some point from which to begin any history of the crisis of the late Republic. We too have been faced with the choice of a starting point and, in this first section, have decided to concentrate on the century leading up to the outbreak of civil war in 49 BC. This is justified not only by the emergence during that period of unprecedented circumstances, but also (as we shall see) by the development of new and destructive combinations of problems and reactions, which individually are firmly rooted in the history and traditions of Republican Rome.

The political revolution—a comparison

Our first problem, then, is to understand the nature of the changes in the political life of Rome between the mid-second and the mid-first century BC. Let us compare the situation around 150 BC with that around 50 BC. The transformation is astonishing. In a hundred years the character of political competition—as well as its potential rewards—changed dramatically. In the 50s, at the very top of the political tree, the prize was total indefinite dominance. Caesar and Pompey fought to rule the Roman world. Contrast the 150s. Then the prizes were of limited character and duration: a consulship, with a colleague, for a year; maybe a second consulship; a short-term command against a foreign enemy. Political methods also changed. Rome in the mid-second century may not have been the haven of communal peace some scholars suggest, but certainly political aims were not then generally pursued through deliberate acts of violence—a complete contrast with the 50s, when political clashes often led to fighting in the city and many were killed.[2]

Rome's character as a 'city-state' also changed beyond recognition. In 150 Rome was already a state whose territory covered much of Italy and whose citizens were ten times more numerous than those of fifth-century Athens. But it was still recognisably related to the classical model of the 'city-state'—with a citizen body characteristically drawn

2. For the tenor of political life in the mid-second century, see Astin, *Scipio*, 1-124 and F.Millar, 'The Political Character of the Classical Roman Republic, 200-151 BC', *JRS* 74 (1984), 1-19. The violence of political life in Rome is clearly characterized by Lintott, *Violence*, esp. 175-203 and 209-216; but note the contrasting interpretation of W.Nippel, 'Policing Rome', *JRS* 74 (1984), 20-29. A.N.Sherwin-White, 'Violence in Roman Politics', *JRS* 46 (1956), 1-9 (repr, in Seager, *Crisis*, 151-159) is largely concerned with the threat of Roman armies to the internal politics of the city, and overestimates the degree of continuity between the middle and late Republic.

from the adult male inhabitants of the urban centre and a (more or less) restricted territory round about. By 50 Rome had entirely transcended such limits. After a brutal war, full citizenship had been granted to Rome's Italian allies. Rome was now Italy, and Italy Rome. Rome no longer bore any resemblance to a 'city-state' in the traditional sense. A similar dramatic change is evident in Rome's position overseas. In 150 Rome was a major power in the Mediterranean, with the beginnings of an overseas empire in the provinces of Sicily, Sardinia, Corsica and Spain. A hundred years later, Rome was a power of almost total predominance, with provincial territory stretching from Gaul to the shores of the Black Sea. The affairs of Rome were the affairs of the whole Mediterranean—as is vividly symbolised by the death of Pompey in 48. Protagonist in a Roman civil war, he met his end on the shores of Egypt.[3]

Problems of explanation

To highlight the transformation in this way is easy. It is more difficult to explain or even describe the process by which the changes occurred. Two points of historical method need emphasis. First, a detailed narrative of the period, which simply presents its readers with a chronological series of events (the tribunate of X, the consulship of Y, the passing of this law, the repeal of that) is not necessarily the most useful for understanding causes or major trends. Day-to-day developments in history are confusing, determined seemingly by chance or the passing ambitions of individuals. The task of the historian, with the help of hindsight, is to impose some structure onto the mass of evidence and construct out of it some sense. So in the remainder of this section, we present one possible framework for plotting the political developments of the late Republic. It is only one of many such frameworks and has no unique claim to being correct. Indeed, in areas such as this, 'correctness' is hard to assess; it is more profitable to ask 'How *helpful* is this scheme in making sense of conflicting and fragmentary evidence?'

The second point concerns explanation. This is more difficult than

3. The classical model of the Greek 'city-state' (*polis*) is well discussed by M.I.Finley, *The Ancient Economy* (London, 1973) esp. 123-149. For a more detailed treatment, see M.I.Finley, 'The Ancient City: from Fustel de Coulanges to Max Weber and beyond', *CSSH* 19 (1977), 305-327 (repr. in Finley, *Economy and Society*, 3-23). For a simpler characterization, see M.M.Austin and P. Vidal-Naquet, *Economic and Social History of Ancient Greece: an Introduction* (London, 1977), 49-53, 78-81. Roman expansion and the war with the allies is discussed below, pp. 72-84.

it may seem at first sight. Philosophically the problem is complicated. Each explanation one proffers raises fresh questions: C causes D, but what causes C?[4] For our practical purposes, it is certain that we cannot explain everything and that there is no single answer to the problems of the late Republic nor any easily traceable chain of causation—one event leading to another leading to the collapse of the Republican political system. Indeed, rather than universal explanation, a more modest, yet more appropriate aim for the historian of the late Republic is 'analytic description'. This attempts to demonstrate how a whole network of factors are closely interlinked, how they cumulatively alter the character of the political process and how that changed character in turn adds new elements to the network. Consider, for example, some of the various elements associated with the growth of Rome's empire. In the first half of the second century BC, with armies recruited among the Italian peasantry, the Romans fought a series of staggeringly successful wars of conquest. As a result, riches flowed into Rome and military victory came to seem more and more profitable and desirable to the Roman governing class. Yet, in order to invest this wealth, the Roman elite dispossessed Italian peasants from their land. They thereby reduced the number of available soldiers and made it more difficult for themselves to pursue wars of conquest. At the same time (as booty did in fact come also to some members of the lower orders) popular perception of the rewards of victory led to ever increasing pressure for further wars. Such an intricate series of structures cannot be fully discussed in the brief compass of this survey; but it underlies much of what we have to say in this and later sections.[5]

A descriptive framework

The starting point of our descriptive framework for the crisis of the Roman Republic is one of the most commonly cited turning points in Roman history—the tribunate of Tiberius Gracchus in 133 BC and of his brother Gaius in 123-122 BC. In what senses was Roman political activity crucially changed by the events of those years?

The course of Tiberius' year in office is familiar: his proposal to

4. For a recognition of problems of this type in the writing of Roman history, see Hopkins, *Conquerors and Slaves*, esp. ix-xi. More generally, note R. F. Atkinson, *Knowledge and Explanation in History: an Introduction to the Philosophy of History* (London, 1978).
5. See, especially, pp. 5-8, 70-71 and 72-77. A useful illustration of complexity may be found in Hopkins, *Conquerors and Slaves*, 1-98 (note the evocative flow-chart, p.12).

distribute illegally occupied public land to the landless poor; his presentation of the proposal to the popular assembly instead of to the senate; the deposition from office of a tribune who opposed the measure; the proposal (again through the popular assembly) to use the revenues from the newly acquired province of Asia to finance the settlements; the attempt to gain a second consecutive tribunate and the violence which ended with Tiberius' murder by a posse of senators and their attendants. Many of these actions, individually, had precedents or constitutional justification; yet the new combination found in the aims and methods of Tiberius was distinctive.[6]

Part of this distinctiveness lay in the formulation of a new role in politics for the Roman people—a role at the same time more powerful and more subject to exploitation. By his use of the popular assembly, Tiberius gave that body the status of rival to the senate as a source, not of political initiative (for that was never encouraged among the citizens at large), but of political authority. Closely linked with this, the proposal concerning the Asian revenues carried with it the implication that the people had some claim on the management of the fruits of the growing empire. Yet these actions also set a precedent for a new pattern of activity by individual politicians; as members of the governing class, in opposition to the senate, exploited in their struggle (cynically or not—we cannot tell) a loaded appeal to public opinion. The tribunate of Tiberius (and of his brother Gaius), by enhancing the authority of the people, had the effect also of making it a more useful political tool.

During these years we also find clearly defined for the first time a politico-economic package that lay behind many conflicts in the late Republic. A major reason for Tiberius' land distribution lay in the problem of army recruitment. Traditionally, legionary soldiers were recruited among men who possessed some land. In the middle of the second century, as a result of prolonged campaigning overseas, many peasants had become impoverished and so had fallen below the level required for military service (see pp. 42-43). Land distribution obviously offered the possibility of restoring some men to the necessary level.

6. A clear narrative of the background and events of Tiberius' tribunate is given by Astin, *Scipio*, 161-241 and by Stockton, *The Gracchi*. An account of the main issues and controversies may be found in E. Badian, 'Tiberius Gracchus and the Beginning of the Roman Revolution', *ANRW* I, 1 (1972), 668-731 (but note the same author's earlier and briefer survey, 'Gracchi to Sulla', esp. 6-20). For a focus of recent debate (on the main motives behind Tiberius' reforms), see Earl, *Tiberius Gracchus*, with the review by P.A.Brunt, *Gnomon* 37 (1965), 189-192. Precedents for 'reforming tribunes' are discussed by L.R.Taylor, 'Forerunners of the Gracchi', *JRS* 52 (1962), 19-27.

Thus Tiberius' legislation introduced into the centre of urban politics a nexus of problems inextricably connected—the poor, the land, the army, the empire. This nexus was to provide the theme for much of the disruption of the next hundred years.[7]

The most radical development of 133, however, lay in the eruption of violence. In a semi-official capacity, a group of senators, without any precedent, put Tiberius (and many of his supporters) to death. A pattern of political action (and reaction) was thus set for the future; and indeed Gaius met the same fate in 121.[8]

Modern scholars have often cast Gaius simply in a supporting role to Tiberius. But this ignores the important innovations of his double tribunate in 123-122. Elected, unlike his brother, to a second term, in two years he proposed a vast amount of legislation. This not only went beyond Tiberius' land law in heralding other major themes of later controversy (the planting of colonies, state-subsidised wheat rations, extension of Roman citizenship more widely in Italy, the establishment of juries which excluded senators to try cases of extortion in the provinces), but also represented a new development simply because it was a major *programme* of reform, depending on the initiative of a single individual. Such personal predominance constituted a threat to the notional equality of the Roman political elite and to its collective control over its individual members. This threat was often repeated in the next two generations.[9]

The Gracchan land distributions did not, in fact, solve the problem of army recruitment.[10] Another approach, however, was possible and

7. The relationship between the land and the army is discussed by Brunt, 'The Army and the Land', and Hopkins, *Conquerors and Slaves*, 1-98. For land-holding and agricultural practice in Italy at the time of the Gracchi, see D.W.Rathbone, 'The Development of Agriculture in the Ager Cosanus during the Roman Republic: Problems of Evidence and Interpretation', *JRS* 71 (1981), 10-23 and M.W.Frederiksen, 'The Contribution of Archaeology to the Agrarian Problem in the Gracchan Period', *DdA* 4-5 (1970-71), 330-367 (stressing the difficulties of drawing conclusions from the available archaeological evidence). The classic study of A.J.Toynbee (*Hannibal's Legacy*, vol. 2 (Oxford, 1965), whose main conclusions are set out in 'Economic and Social Consequences of the Hannibalic War', *Bull.J.Ryl.Lib.* 37 (1954-55), 271-287) exaggerates the extent to which peasant farmers had disappeared from Italy by the time of the Gracchi. See further on peasants, P.Garnsey, 'Peasants in Ancient Roman Society', *Journal of Peasant Studies* 3 (1976), 221-235.
8. Fully discussed by Lintott, *Violence*, 175-183.
9. Unlike most modern accounts, Stockton, *The Gracchi* gives due consideration to the work of Gaius. For a detailed chronology (and interpretation) of Gaius' measures in relation to the allies, see Badian, *Foreign Clientelae*, 185-186, 299-301; for his measures concerning the jury courts (particularly the extortion court), E.Badian, 'Lex Acilia Repetundarum', *AJPh* 75 (1954), 374-384 and A.N.Sherwin-White, 'The Lex Repetundarum and the Political Ideas of Gaius Gracchus', *JRS* 72 (1982), 18-31.
10. The commission for land distribution set up by Tiberius remained in operation

had from time to time since the third century been adopted. The reserve of recruits could be increased by lowering the property level required. This process reached its logical conclusion in 107, when Marius openly enrolled men into his army with no regard for property qualification whatever. Modern scholars recognise that Marius did no more than recruit *openly* among the poorest class, who had in practice (though strictly illegally) been enrolled before. However, historians in antiquity (as, for example, Sallust) perceived his actions as a clear break with tradition.[11]

Important consequences followed. Soldiers who lacked wealth and property in Italy necessarily rested all their hopes on military service and, in particular, relied on their general to secure them land on retirement. The general, in turn, was encouraged to enter the political arena to provide for his men; and found himself in that arena with an armed force owing him personal loyalty. This was a dangerous interdependence, which quickly proved explosive. Witness the wave of violence that erupted when Saturninus, as tribune of the people in 103 and 100, attempted to provide for distributions of land to Marius' veterans.[12]

The dangerous character of Roman 'professional' armies was further revealed during the war between Rome and her Italian allies (the *socii*), commonly known as the 'Social War' (91-88). We shall return to this in a later section (pp. 80-82), and note here just two aspects. First, in all essentials the soldiers were fighting a civil war. Over the past two hundred years, Romans and Italians (often linked by ties of kinship) had fought side by side against foreign enemies. Now they turned against each other. This was one step nearer a war in which Roman

---

only until 119/111 BC. Traces of parts of the distribution still survive in the inscribed landmarkers (*cippi*) set up by the commission: see *ILLRP* 467-475, with the illustrations in *ILLRP, Imagines*, 199-200. The effect of the distributions on the number of citizens eligible for military service (as reflected in the Roman census returns) is discussed by Brunt, *Italian Manpower*, 75-83.

11. For the ancient view, see Sallust, *Jugurthine War* 86. The 'reform' of army recruitment is fully discussed by Hopkins, *Conquerors and Slaves*, esp. 25-37 and by Brunt, 'The Army and the Land'; and, more technically, by Gabba, *Republican Rome*, 1-19 ('The Origins of the Professional Army at Rome: the 'Proletarii' and Marius' Reform') and Brunt, *Italian Manpower*, 391-415. J.W.Rich ('The Supposed Roman Manpower Shortage of the Later Second Century BC', *Historia* 32 (1983), 287-331) has attempted to go against the traditional view and to suggest that the Romans were experiencing no problems of recruitment. His arguments are not finally convincing, but do demonstrate the inadequacy of the ancient evidence on this issue.

12. Note that Marius has also been regarded as a champion of the 'equestrian order' (on which, see below, pp. 44-47). This view—hard to substantiate on the available evidence—is clearly expressed by Badian, *Foreign Clientelae*, 195-196, 201-202, 233-234.

fought Roman. Secondly, the Roman armies raised for this conflict were more than ever before 'private' armies. The soldiers recruited by Cnaeus Pompeius Strabo effectively belonged to him, and in this they resembled the troops of later dynasts (his son Pompey, Caesar and the others), who would fight on behalf of their own general against the common interest of Rome. Indeed, when Crassus remarked that no one might be called wealthy who could not pay an army out of his fortune, he gave evidence not only of the immense riches of the Roman leaders, but also of the political methods they might countenance.[13]

The career of Sulla (c.138-78) brought the culmination of this erosion of scruples and of the other trends we have isolated. Refusing to accept the transfer to the now elderly Marius of his command in the war against King Mithridates VI of Pontus in the east, he got his army behind him, marched on Rome and took the city after a few hours' fighting. This was civil war in essence and in name; and the violence was repeated, in yet worse form, when he returned to Italy from victory in the east. His army had been used in a way (as we see with hindsight) that was only too predictable. Predictable too was Sulla's establishment of his position as 'dictator'. Relying not on any of the standard magistracies, but on special office, he reached a predominance foreshadowed but not attained by earlier leaders, such as Gaius Gracchus or Marius.[14]

The period from Sulla to the Civil War in 49 is one of the best documented in all Roman history. Ironically though, most preconditions for devastating internal conflict had already been set and we see fewer crucial developments than in the previous two generations, but rather a gradual further loosening of restraint.[15] Let us consider four aspects of interest.

13. The brutality of the 'Social War' and the conflict between one-time friends is well illustrated by Diodorus of Sicily, *The Library of History*, 37, 15 (written c.60-30 BC). For the 'private' army of Cn. Pompeius Strabo, see Badian, *Foreign Clientelae*, 227-229, 234. The wealth of Crassus and other Roman senators is discussed by I.Shatzman, *Senatorial Wealth and Roman Politics* (Coll. Lat. 142, Brussels, 1975), esp. 375-378 (on Crassus). The quip of Crassus on financing an army is recorded by Cicero, *Stoic Paradoxes* 43 and Pliny, *Natural History* 33, 47, 134.

14. For a concise and clear narrative of Sulla's career, see Badian, *Foreign Clientelae*, 230-251. This forms a more reliable guide than the highly personal views put forward by the same author in 'Waiting for Sulla', *JRS* 52 (1962), 47-61 (repr. in Badian, *Studies*, 206-234) and *Lucius Sulla: the Deadly Reformer* (Sydney, 1970). On various aspects of Sulla's reforms, see Gabba, *Republican Rome*, 131-141 ('Drusus and Sulla's Reforms') and 142-150 ('The Equestrian Class and Sulla's Senate'); Brunt, *Italian Manpower*, 300-312 (on the effects of the colonies of Sulla's veterans established in Italy).

15. The comparative wealth of evidence for the final period of the Republic has encouraged a spate of biographies of the leading figures. In general, such stress on the

First, considerable political attention was focussed on the tribunate. Among Sulla's measures was an attempt to deprive the tribunate of its strength and power. Then for ten years this was an issue of conflict, until gradually all the prerogatives of the tribunes were restored. The political energy expended on this conflict may now seem misdirected, in that the final civil war of the Republic was, in crude terms, brought about not by tribunes, but by generals and their armies. Yet tribunes did, in fact, play an important supporting role in this final phase of the Republic. Their traditional relationship with the Roman people meant that they became closely linked to the great military commanders. For it was they who often proposed the laws that granted generals their commands; they also frequently aided a returning general by introducing legislation to provide land for his troops.[16]

Secondly, the power and influence wielded by individual politicians was greater than ever before. As a result, apparently traditional behaviour led to quite untraditional consequences. So, when Pompey, Caesar and Crassus made their compact in 60 in the face of various kinds of opposition, political life at Rome changed. Such deals had, of course, been made before—but the combined wealth and power of these men was unprecedented. Hence they could dominate Roman political processes. From this compact stems directly further violence and, according to some, the civil war of 49.[17]

---

careers of individuals (well-documented, in fact, only in patches) does not provide the most helpful entry into the problems of the period; however, for beginners, J.Leach, *Pompey the Great* (London, 1978) and W.K.Lacey, *Cicero and the End of the Roman Republic* (London, etc., 1978) provide an accurate narrative and set their subject in a wider context. For a sober account of Cicero's political career (the best documented of all), see Stockton, *Cicero*. Many individual essays on specific topics relating to the first century BC are referred to below. For the moment, note the following books largely concerned with political life in the final phase of the Republic: Gruen, *Last Generation*; Syme, *Roman Revolution*; Taylor, *Party Politics*. An extensive bibliography on the late Republic is contained within the notes of Scullard, *Gracchi to Nero*.
16. Note, for example, the relationship between Pompey's command in the East and the action of tribunes at Rome: the bill granting him command against Mithridates was introduced in 66 BC by the tribune C. Manilius (see Cicero's speech, *On the Command of Pompey*); on his return in 60 BC, another tribune, Flavius, introduced a bill to provide land for his veterans (see Dio, *Histories* 37, 49-50; Cicero, *Letters to Atticus* 1, 18 (Shackleton Bailey 18), 16; 1, 19 (Shackleton Bailey 19), 4. The tribunates of particular men have attracted special attention. For Clodius (tribune 58), see E.S.Gruen, 'P. Clodius Pulcher, Instrument or Independent Agent?', *Phoenix* 20 (1966), 120-130; A.W.Lintott, 'P. Clodius Pulcher—*Felix Catilina*?', *G&R* 14 (1967), 157-169. For Curio (tribune 50), see W.K.Lacey, 'The Tribunate of Curio', *Historia* 10 (1961), 318-329. But note that men of this kind are the exceptions among the ten tribunes elected each year: see below, p. 65, for the office of tribune in general.
17. Syme, *Roman Revolution* (following Asinius Pollio in placing the origin of the Civil War in 60 BC) demonstrates the significance of the compact in the breakdown of the

A third point of interest lies in the appeals that were increasingly made by many of the Roman elite to the principles of *collective* rule—even in the face of overwhelming challenges to those principles. The writings of Cicero provide many examples of this, as do also the discussions in the senate in the months immediately before the outbreak of war in 49. Most senators did not accept that conflict was inevitable, but voted that Pompey and Caesar should both give up their armies and subordinate themselves to collective rule. This kind of expression formed, on one level, a strong counterpoint to the claims of individual dynasts. But, on another level, the urgency of such appeals in fact suggests that the credibility of the state was by this time seen to be in doubt.[18]

Finally, we should emphasise the process by which Rome became familiarised with the situation revealed by the actions of Sulla. If the preconditions of the collapse of the Republic are evident to us already in the 80s, there was little sign yet that Romans could capitalise on them. Sulla had gone beyond what was acceptable: all his officers but one deserted him on the march to Rome and he himself only retained his position as 'dictator' for a few months. Thirty-five years later, when Caesar invaded Italy, all but one of his officers stayed with him and when he became 'dictator' the office rapidly became permanent. What had changed? In the first place it is clear that some form of predominance had become regularised in the series of 'special commands' that were granted during this period. Traditional office-holding, with limited term and limited power, could not deal with the problems of a large empire and the elite was forced to accept, for instance, that the cost of clearing the seas of pirates was that the commander involved was officially granted money, troops and powers which elevated him way above his peers. Secondly, the example of Pompey was of particular importance. His early career, built entirely upon military success, culminated in 71: outside Rome and in command of his army, he obtained from the senate (no doubt with the unspoken threat of violent

---

Republic; see, especially pp. 8-9 and 35-38. A vivid symbol of the dominance of the three men is found in the so-called 'Conference of Luca': when Caesar, Pompey and Crassus met in North Italy in 56 BC to patch up their differences, 200 senators are said to have made the journey to attend on their discussions (Plutarch, *Life of Pompey* 51, 3; *Life of Caesar* 21, 2).

18. The second book of Cicero's *On the Republic* provides a clear example of an appeal to the traditional principles of collective rule. Written in the late 50s, but set (as a dialogue) in 129 BC, it reviews the history of Rome as a model of the ideal state. For the senatorial vote in December 50 (in which 370 voted that both men should give up their armies, with only 22 against), see Appian, *Civil Wars* 2, 30.

intervention) permission to stand for a consulship before holding any other elected office, and a triumph. He proceeded later in the east to yet more striking forms of dominance, acting frequently without reference to the senate and occupying an almost royal position: coins were minted carrying his portrait; cities were named after him; religious cult was offered to him. Away from Rome, Pompey had gone far beyond what might now seem the tentative steps of Sulla. It was left only for Caesar, after the civil war, to apply these principles in Rome itself.[19]

19. On the system of 'special commands', see Crawford, *Roman Republic*, 203-204, and note the survey of R.T.Ridley, 'The Extraordinary Commands of the Late Republic: a Matter of Definition', *Historia* 30 (1981), 280-297 (though in our view he underestimates the innovation which these commands represented). The special position of Pompey is highlighted by Crawford, *Roman Republic*, 176-178 and F.Millar, *The Emperor in the Roman World* (London, 1977), 611-612. For reference to the eastern coins and inscriptions honouring Pompey, see M.H.Crawford, 'Hamlet without the Prince' (review of Gruen, *Last Generation*), *JRS* 66 (1976), 216 or S.Weinstock, *Divus Julius* (Oxford, 1971), 154, 184 n.5, 197. The position of Caesar is discussed below, pp. 185-186.

Chapter Two

THE CULTURAL HORIZONS OF
THE ARISTOCRACY

Modern accounts of the Roman Republic tend to place its cultural and religious history at the margins. The reason for this is partly a very restricted notion of what subjects constitute 'history' (elections, wars, treaties, rather than literature, art, patterns of thought); but it is also partly an uncertainty about how culture and religion should be handled by historians. Since they cannot simply be absorbed into political history, it has often seemed easiest to relegate them to the background, occasionally to enliven a dull political narrative (70 BC: Pompey's first consulship, Virgil born), but not seriously to encroach on the 'real centre' of action.

In fact, an understanding of the cultural developments of the last period of the Roman Republic and of the patterning of its religious mentality is of central importance. History is not merely about events and actions, but also about how they were perceived and discussed. The development, for example, of moral and political philosophy in the late Republic, bringing with it new ways for the Roman governing class to understand and justify their own conduct, is just as important as the political events themselves. For this reason we have chosen to take as our first themes these two fundamental areas: culture and religion. Each one demands slightly different chronological limits; in this chapter we will start with the very beginnings of a literary tradition in Latin—the late third century BC.[1]

In the field of culture the last two centuries of the Republic were centuries of rapid change. We tend to take for granted the literature of the age of Cicero: the verses of Catullus, the histories of Sallust, the philosophical poem of Lucretius, the vast range of literary output from Cicero himself—public speeches, treatises on rhetoric and

---

1. For the moral framework within which the Roman elite operated, see Earl, *Political Tradition*, 1-43.

philosophy, autobiographical poetry and much more. Yet less than two hundred years before Cicero literary production in Latin was something new, barely extending beyond translations of, or adaptations from, Greek epic poetry and drama and the first pioneering attempts by Romans at the creation of 'original' epics, dramas, speeches, histories. Maturity and diversity (consider also Roman satire, technical writing on agriculture, law, grammar and so on) came with remarkable speed. It was similar with the visual arts and architecture. In the late Republic we start to find portrait sculpture in considerable quantity with a recognisably 'Roman' style; at the same time, there were striking advances in building and urban planning. Witness the lavish development around the temple of Fortuna at Praeneste (a few miles outside Rome): a massive complex of linked terraces, colonnades, ramps and a theatre was built on the hillside above (and completely dominating) the small existing town. This was just one of the schemes through which the appearance of Italian cities and rural sanctuaries was transformed.[2]

The catalyst in this process was Rome's direct contact with Greece. Of course, throughout her history, Rome had been open to influence from the Greek settlements of South Italy and from her partially Hellenized neighbours, the Etruscans; but this was nothing compared with that contact which started in the late third century, when Rome's imperial ambitions took her into the eastern Mediterranean and the Greek world itself. There members of the governing class gained first-hand acquaintance with the cultural apparatus which made Greece distinctively different from Rome—traditions of abstract thinking, artistic skills and literary achievements in fields as diverse as love poetry and astronomy.[3]

The result was a complex process of cultural integration, which has often been misinterpreted or oversimplified by modern scholars. In particular, it has been common practice to ignore the importance of Roman culture simply because it can be portrayed as a pale shadow of its Greek

2. For an introduction to the history of Roman literature in the Republic, see R.M.Ogilvie, *Roman Literature and Society* (Harmondsworth, 1980), 11-160. A more detailed survey is provided by the *Cambridge History of Classical Literature* 2, 53-294, with up to date bibliographies on all the authors mentioned here, pp. 799-846. The sections on the earliest Republican literature by A.S.Gratwick (pp. 53-171) are especially useful and should be referred to (even when not specifically mentioned in our notes) throughout the first part of this chapter. For art and architecture, see Bianchi Bandinelli, *Rome*; Strong, *Roman Art* (less good on historical context and interpretation); A.Boethius, *Etruscan and Early Roman Architecture* (rev. R.Ling and T.Rasmussen, Harmondsworth, 1978) (for the development at Praeneste, see esp. pp. 168-174).
3. For a short general account of the process, see Wardman, *Rome's Debt to Greece*.

ancestor. If Plato, for example, was a 'better' philosopher than Cicero, why should we be at all interested in the work of the latter? Such crude comparisons are, of course, absurd—rather like ignoring the architecture of St Paul's Cathedral on the grounds that it does not match the standard of the Parthenon. We feel certain that Roman literature, art and thought are better seen within their own historical context and as vital elements in a period of striking cultural transformation.[4]

The speed and character of this process of transformation were determined by the conduct and attitudes of the Roman governing class— their wealth and competitiveness one with another. With expansion into the Greek world, the Roman elite not only saw for the first time what Greek culture had to offer; they also won, through conquest, wealth on such a staggering scale that they could obtain for themselves whatever they wanted—works of art or the services of Greek artists and intellectuals. A widening of Roman cultural ambitions coincided exactly with the influx in wealth which enabled those ambitions to be fulfilled. Yet, in addition to this coincidence, momentum was given to the process of cultural development by the competitive ethos prevailing among the Roman elite. They were notionally equals—but also rivals. If one man temporarily outstripped his peers, the rest had no option but to follow suit and catch up or lose face (and status) by comparison. This competition proved explosive in the field of politics; yet it gave to the process of Hellenization at Rome an extraordinary dynamic. For precedents (in the acquisition of literary skills or works of art) once set by one member of the elite were necessarily followed by the others.

Attempts were made to check this cultural innovation and the conspicuous displays of wealth that went with it. In the second century BC the elder Cato (234-149), in particular, stood out against many facets of Hellenization. Yet the usefulness of what Greek culture had to offer in the competitive milieu of the Roman elite was too great to allow any serious opposition to its assimilation. Indeed, even Cato himself could not, in practice, remain unaffected by it. The evidence of his own writings demonstrates that he was well acquainted with things Greek and influenced by them; not only do the surviving fragments of his speeches show a familiarity with Greek rhetorical theory, but

4. We therefore disagree radically with the approach exemplified by L.P.Wilkinson, in *Cambridge History of Classical Literature* 2, 265. For Wilkinson, the philosophy of Cicero is 'significant', principally because it preserved some awareness of the substance of Greek philosophy in Western Europe through the Middle Ages, when knowledge of the Greek language had practically died out.

in many of his works he makes pointed reference to passages of Greek literature.[5]

In considering the stages of cultural development at Rome against this general background, we have to be schematic. Cultural development does not actually happen in neatly defined phases, nor does literature always develop in parallel with art and architecture. Nevertheless the three stages we outline should provide a helpful framework for making some historical sense of the vast profusion of literary and material culture of the late Republic.

The starting point for the developments in literature, on the one hand, and art, on the other, must be distinguished. It is striking that the literary tradition of the late Republic did not emerge from a native primitive strand of Latin literature. While there are a few scanty traces of a crude native dramatic tradition, there was no early development of, for example, epic or ballad. The Romans had nothing comparable with the *Iliad*, *Odyssey* or *Beowulf*. Essentially Roman literature started from cold in the second half of the third century BC.[6]

With art and architecture the position is different. From very early in their history, along with their Etruscan neighbours, the Romans had built houses and temples, made pottery and metalwork. Indeed some fine terracotta statuary of the sixth century BC still survives. To some extent such works of art provide a background against which to see later developments. Yet there is a break. For it is only in the third century BC that we may properly speak of specifically *Roman* developments in art, determined by *Rome's* growing contact with Greece. Unlike literature, art existed in Rome before our period, but it had then no status independent of Rome's neighbours.[7]

Translation

The first of our three stages of Roman cultural development is that

5. See Astin, *Cato*, especially 157-181; Crawford, *Roman Republic*, 85-89; and for a clear discussion of the Character of Cato's oratory, A.S.Gratwick, in *Cambridge History of Classical Literature* 2, 152.
6. The most judicious account of the 'Atellan farces' and other alleged early Latin 'literature' is that in H.J.Rose, *A Handbook of Latin Literature* (3rd ed., London, 1954) 1-19 and 22-6; see also the difficult, but rewarding article of A.D.Momigliano, 'Perizonius, Niebuhr and the Character of Early Roman Tradition', *JRS* 47 (1957), 104-114 (repr. in *Essays in Ancient and Modern Historiography* (Oxford, 1977), 231-251).
7. For an illustrated account of early Republican art and architecture in its Italian context (though rather dated in its interpretation), see R.Bloch, *The Origins of Rome* (London, 1960); a number of recent Italian exhibition catalogues spectacularly increases the range of illustrative material available: *Civiltà del Lazio Primitivo* (Rome, 1976); *Prima*

of translation from the Greek—exemplified by the work of L.Livius Andronicus (? c.290-c.205), a man of South Italian Greek origin and the first author known to have written in Latin. Although only small fragments of his writings survive, we know that they included Latin translations of Homer's *Odyssey* and of various Greek dramas. However 'free' these were, their effect was to begin to make available to the Romans what were then the established genres of Greek literature— epic poetry, tragedy and comedy. More recondite areas of Greek literature were discovered later.[8]

'Translation' in this sense was not, of course, necessary for works of art; but a similar process of development is represented by the first influx of art objects as booty from Roman conquests in the Greek world. As early as the 270s, Manius Curius Dentatus, after a successful campaign in the Greek area of South Italy, brought back to Rome major works of Greek sculpture—thus beginning the process of familiarising the Romans with Greek artistic masterpieces.[9]

This concern with translation, by itself, did not last long. Yet throughout the Republic and beyond, translation remained as one significant element, alongside more complex and original forms of cultural production. Cicero, for example, who was, on the one hand, strikingly innovative in developing a distinctively Roman philosophical tradition, also produced a verse paraphrase of a Greek poem on astronomy (Aratus' *Phaenomena*) and, like many of his peers, continued to import into Italy—or make copies of—original Greek works of art.[10]

Adaptation

The next phase of cultural development was closely linked to the particular concerns of the Roman elite. For, beyond translation, cultural adaptation and innovation soon occurred in those areas where literature

---

Italia: arts Italiques du premier millénaire avant J.C. (Brussels, 1980 = Rome, 1981); *Enea nel Lazio: archeologia e mito* (Rome, 1981).

8. For references to translations of the work of Livius Andronicus (and other authors mentioned in this chapter), see our Appendix, pp. 88-90.

9. See Pollitt, *Art of Rome*, 32-48 (for translations of ancient sources documenting Roman plundering of works of art); and J.J.Pollitt, 'The Impact of Greek Art on Rome', *TAPhA* 108 (1978), 155-174.

10. For Cicero's translation of Aratus' poem, see G.B.Townend, 'The Poems', in T.A.Dorey (ed.), *Cicero* (London, 1965), esp. 112-117; on translation in general, Williams, *Tradition and Originality*, 251-67, abridged in *Nature of Roman Poetry*, 55-7; on the continued importation and copying of Greek works of art, see Pollitt, *Art of Rome*, 74-81; Strong, *Roman Art*, 25-31.

and art could serve the needs (collective or individual) of the governing class.

The development of history writing from the late third century provides a clear example of this. Heavily involved in the Greek world, the Roman elite now faced, as adversaries or allies, communities with a developed sense of their own past and a strong feeling of identity. The Romans now needed (as a group) publicity framed in terms understandable to the Greeks—they needed to project a 'history'. The work of Quintus Fabius Pictor, a Roman senator who around 200 wrote in Greek the first prose account of Roman history, was a response to those needs; so also was the slightly later history of Lucius Cincius Alimentus, likewise written in Greek. Neither of these works, unfortunately, survives beyond small fragments quoted in later authors.[11]

A different collective need was answered by Cato's *Origines*, a Latin history written in the mid-second century. In addition to the history of Rome, this work included accounts of the origins of the different communities in Italy—reflecting an awareness that Rome was increasingly assimilating the whole of Italy into its sphere. Not directed at the Greek world, the *Origines* are a product of the concern of the Roman aristocracy to understand their position within the changing world about them.[12]

Other, individual, needs were fulfilled by works of history. Cato's *Origines*, for example, may also be seen in an individual context. For the author inserted passages from his own speeches—thus publicising his own views. Other historians used their writing to glorify their ancestors—which in turn served to advertise the status of living members of their family. A similar purpose may be detected in the historical epic poem of Quintus Ennius (239-169)—the *Annales*—a work later regarded as the inspiration for all Latin epic. While in part this represented a celebration of the aristocratic virtues of the governing class as a whole, it also served in part to glorify the poet's aristocratic patron, Quintus Fulvius Nobilior.[13]

The early prominence of other forms of literature—especially drama and oratory—may be understood in broadly similar terms. The comedies of Plautus (who died in or after 184), Terence (c.190-159) and

11. For a clear discussion of the early historians, see Badian, 'Early Historians'.
12. See Astin, *Cato*, 211-239.
13. On the role of literature in the celebration of aristocratic virtues, see Earl, *Political Tradition*, 11-43. Fabius Pictor's glorification of his own family in his history is discussed by Badian, 'Early Historians', 2-7. On the treatment of one particular family (the Claudii) in Roman history writing, see Wiseman, *Clio's Cosmetics*, 55-139, with the important review by T.J.Cornell, *JRS* 72 (1982), 203-206.

other early dramatists, free adaptations of Greek plays, served collective and individual ends: they were staged at festivals as part of public acts of worship, but they also brought glory to the individual magistrate who was responsible for the festival and paid for the dramatist. Serious drama could have an even more striking individual element—for some plays simply used the form (not the plot) of a Greek tragedy to celebrate the deeds of famous Romans. Thus Pacuvius (c.220-c.130) wrote a play celebrating the victory of Lucius Aemilius Paullus over the King of Macedonia in 168.[14]

The rise of oratory may also be related to the needs of the Roman elite. Not only could the texts of speeches be used to publicise the views of individual politicians, but, as political competition became fiercer through the second century, higher value was placed on (originally) Greek rhetorical techniques which added to the force and persuasiveness of public speaking.[15]

In architecture and the visual arts similarly, development first occurred where it was of service to the elite. A splendid public building could represent a permanent memorial to a man's prestige and could help the standing of his descendants for generations. So, much of the wealth won in the east went into building at Rome and other central Italian towns. Temples, porticoes, basilicas were erected, often under the supervision of Greek architects. We can see clearly in the series of temples built in the second century Greek architecture adapted to a Roman context. Elements of the traditional, simple Italic temple remained—but now monumentalised through fusion with a range of Greek features: flanking colonnades, stuccoed columns in the Greek architectural orders, occasional use of fine marble and so on.[16]

---

14. On the blending of Greek and Roman elements in Plautus and Terence, see Williams, *Tradition and Originality*, 285-294 (*Nature of Roman Poetry*, 61-63); W.G.Arnott, *Menander, Plautus, Terence (Greece and Rome* New Survey 9, Oxford, 1975), 28-62; F.H.Sandbach, *The Comic Theatre of Greece and Rome* (London, 1977), 118-147; Williams, 'Political Patronage', discusses the glory accruing to magistrates from the staging of plays (pp.5-7) and the use of *fabulae praetextae* to celebrate the virtues of individual statesmen (pp. 4-5).
15. For the context of Roman oratory, see G.Kennedy, *The Art of Rhetoric in the Roman World* (Princeton, 1972), 3-102. Wardman, *Rome's Debt to Greece*, 111-134 discusses Roman use of Greek rhetorical theory. For ancient discussion, note Cicero's dialogue, *Brutus*—a history of oratory at Rome down to Cicero's own day, and also in effect an intellectual history of the Roman Republic. Fragments of second-century speeches—those of Gaius Gracchus—are collected in Stockton, *The Gracchi*, 217-225; for translations, see *From the Gracchi to Sulla. Sources for Roman History, 133-80 BC* (LACTOR 13, London, 1981), 30-31, 38-39.
16. See F.Coarelli, 'Public Building in Rome between the Second Punic War and Sulla', *PBSR* 32 (1977), 1-23; also, more technically, M.G. Morgan, 'The Portico of Metellus: a Reconsideration', *Hermes* 99 (1971), 480-505. A sense of the political significance of public building comes across both from Velleius Paterculus' (c.19 BC—after AD 30)

On a smaller scale, the designs of Roman coins ('sculpture in minia-ture') from the late second century onwards also demonstrate the use of Greek skill in a specifically Roman context. The technique of coin engraving at Rome certainly owed much to Greek expertise; but the series of strikingly varied and inventive designs towards the close of the second century were stimulated by the competitive political ethos at Rome. For the young officials chosen each year to take charge of the Roman mint found in the coinage a vehicle for self-advertisement—introducing designs that depicted the achievements of their ancestors or alluded to their own political programme and interests. One chose to advertise the bravery of an ancestor in the Second Punic War, another the role of laws passed by earlier mem-bers of his family in securing the protection of ordinary Roman citizens from arbitrary arrest and punishment by the holders of high office.[17]

This close connection between Roman culture and the needs and aspirations of the elite never ceased. Even in the first century, when cultural production had become much more diverse, some works of art and literature were still produced, at least partly, in response to those needs. A good example of this is the first-century development of a distinctively Roman style of portraiture—which quite clearly owed its impetus to the desire of Roman aristocrats to project a public image. Not so obvious, perhaps, is the case of the *Commentarii* written by Caesar—accounts of his campaigns in Gaul and in the civil war against Pompey. Despite first impressions, these were not dispassionate mili-tary narratives, but served to justify the conduct of Caesar and, by celebrating the gallantry of his officers, to advance their careers. Poetry could also fulfil the same function. Indeed, Cicero could claim in a speech delivered in 62, in defence of the poet Archias, that a poet's most important role lay in glorifying the achievements of great men. This was no ludicrous claim—after all, Cicero himself composed a poem in celebration of his glorious consulship.[18]

---

account of the building of the Portico of Metellus (*Histories* 1, 11, 2-5) and from the climax of Cicero's speech *On Behalf of Scaurus* (23, 46-48), in which the orator appeals in his defence of Scaurus to the temples and buildings restored or adorned by Scaurus' ancestors. For the nationality of artists in the Roman world, see J.M.C.Toynbee, *Some Notes on Artists in the Roman World* (Coll. Lat. 6, Brussels, 1951); for a different perspec-tive (Italian artists working in the East), see E.D.Rawson, 'Architecture and Sculpture: the Activities of the Cossutii', *PBSR* 30 (1975), 36-47.
17. M.H.Crawford, *Roman Republican Coinage* (Cambridge, 1974), 712-734 with cata-logue nos. 264 (a coin celebrating the bravery of a moneyer's ancestor) and 301 (refer-ence to an ancestor's legislation); more briefly, note the illustration and commentary in Crawford, *Roman Republic*, Pl. 7.
18. On portraits, see the straightforward account in Walker and Burnett, *Image of*

The cultural explosion

Despite this continuity, the first century BC (and in some respects the end of the second) represents a new stage in cultural development: widespread cultural 'take-off', no longer delimited by the interests of the governing class. The diversity and scale of the achievements of this phase are so vast that we can do no more than isolate some aspects, important for its historical understanding.

First a *caveat*. The explosion of culture did not involve the poor or lower classes, as either producers or consumers. It involved, rather, progressively broader bands of the Roman and Italian elite—and it put at their disposal yet more new types of cultural product: rich floor mosaics for private houses, love poetry, witty or obscene epigrams. The vast majority of Romans were excluded (except as onlookers); for they could neither read nor write, nor afford to decorate their homes. This restriction must constantly be borne in mind.[19]

The most striking development from the late second century on is the growing 'acceptability' of literary activity. On the one hand, it became more an everyday part of the life of an aristocrat. So, a man such as Quintus Lutatius Catulus, consul in 102, could spend part of his leisure not in reading or writing such 'useful' works as history or speeches, but in composing Latin versions of Greek erotic epigrams. On the other hand, lower down the social scale, we find the rise of the independent 'writer'. That is to say, Lucilius (who died in 102 or 101) and Catullus (c.84-54), men of some means, were 'poets', not 'men who happened to write poetry'. As such they were unlike either Quintus Catulus, a senator who wrote poetry, or Ennius, a professional poet in the service of an aristocratic patron. This independent status had, as we shall see, an effect on the kind of writing they produced.[20]

Augustus, 1-14; also Smith, 'Portraiture'. There is a comprehensive bibliography in U.W.Hiesinger, 'Portraiture in the Roman Republic', in *ANRW* 1, 4 , 805-825. A clear example of the political significance of Caesar's *Commentarii* is brought out by T.P.Wiseman, 'The Ambitions of Quintus Cicero', *JRS* 56 (1966), 108-115, esp.114. On Archias, see Wiseman, 'Poets and Patrons', 31-34. A substantial fragment of Cicero's poem on his consulship can be found in the first book of his *On Divination* (11, 17—13, 22).

19. For the living conditions of the Roman poor, see Z.Yavetz, 'The Living Conditions of the Urban Plebs in Republican Rome', *Latomus* 17 (1958), 500-517 (repr.in Seager (ed.), *Crisis*, 162-179). For the rural peasants, R.MacMullen, *Roman Social Relations* (Newhaven and London, 1974), 1-27. On literacy in Rome, see briefly, Finley, *Politics*, 29-31 and, in greater detail, W.V.Harris, 'Literacy and Epigraphy I', *ZPE* 52 (1983), 87-111, with earlier bibliography.

20. Poems of Q.Lutatius Catulus are preserved by Cicero (*On the Nature of the Gods* 1,

In this final period, literary skills became more than ever before a means of penetrating the higher echelons of the Roman elite. In terms of political advancement, the demonstration of rhetorical prowess, leading to success in the courts, could bring an aspiring politician to public notice. This might compensate, as in the case of Cicero, for the lack of a distinguished ancestry—the traditional support in the early stages of a political career. Literary skills could also help in bringing men of the local aristocracies in the Italian towns into the sphere of the governing class in Rome. It is striking how many of the writers of the late Republic actually hailed from outside the capital—Catullus from Verona, Varro from Reate, Cicero from Arpinum and many others. Of course, it was not just literary skills that could bring such men from the Italian towns to Rome; but those skills would have encouraged their migration and provided on their arrival easier access to the milieux of the social and political elite, who shared that literate culture. Catullus was not the only scion of the Veronese well-to-do in Rome in the first century BC, but he was one of the very few that mixed with the top rank of the Roman aristocracy.[21]

Direct contacts with Greek culture also became more intensive, as Greece was fully assimilated into Rome's empire. Tours of duty in the east enabled Roman statesmen to visit the cultural capital of Athens; and young aristocrats often undertook part of their education there. In the opposite direction, more Greek artists and writers became resident in Italy. These had not been entirely absent before. Polybius (c.200-after 118), the historian of Rome's rise to dominance in the Mediterranean, lived for many years in Rome, first as a hostage, later voluntarily. Likewise Panaetius (c.185-109), a philosopher from Rhodes, came to Italy and found a welcome among the same group of aristocrats as had Polybius; and there were other temporary residents. By the first century such men were more numerous and less dependent on the hospitality and patronage of single members of the elite: the poet Archias wrote in honour of Marius, Lucullus and the Metelli, and was defended by Cicero, as we have seen; the sculptor Arcesilaus worked for Lucullus, Varro, Caesar and Pollio.[22]

28, 79) and Aulus Gellius (*Attic Nights* 19, 19, 10); on the rise of the 'professional' poet see Williams, 'Political Patronage' and, for the different social statuses of poets in the Late Republic, Wiseman, 'Poets and Patrons'.
21. For the origins of Cicero and his early career at Rome, see Rawson, *Cicero*, 1-28; T.P.Wiseman discusses Catullus and other Italian authors in '*Domi Nobiles* and the Roman Cultural Elite', in *Les 'Bourgeoisies' municipales italiennes aux IIe et Ier siècles av.J.C.* (Naples, 1983), 299-307.
22. For Romans educated in Athens, see L.W.Daly, 'Roman Study Abroad', *AJPh* 71

Works of literature also travelled. By the first century, many Italian villas—country properties of Roman aristocrats—possessed libraries well-stocked with Greek books. These collections were often the fruit of Rome's eastern conquests—as was Cicero's library, bought from the descendants of Sulla, who had acquired it in the east. These resources, as well as the increased contact with the cultural centres of Greece itself, brought to the Roman elite a familiarity with a much wider range of Greek writing. In the late third century, Roman knowledge extended little beyond Homer, fifth-century Athenian tragedy and the 'new comedy' of Menander and his contemporaries. By the first century, the whole of Greek literature was available to them—philosophy, technical and scientific treatises, later epic poetry, lyric and much more besides. All this necessarily stimulated new areas of Latin writing.[23]

One new area was the writing of Latin philosophy. There had been, admittedly, some Latin philosophical writing before the first century. None of this survives, but it almost certainly consisted in simple didactic accounts of the tenets of the major Greek philosophical 'schools' ('All you ever wanted to know about Stoicism/Epicureanism ...'), with little attempt to relate theory to life in Rome. What marks out much philosophical writing of the first century BC—and especially the surviving treatises of Cicero—is precisely that attempt. For Cicero did not simply present Greek philosophical thought, for its own sake, but used it and adapted it to examine different aspects of Roman life: intellectual history in the *Brutus*; religion in *On Divination*; politics in *On the State*; morals in *On Duties*. Whatever the objective 'quality' of this writing, one should not underestimate the importance of this creative attempt to integrate things Roman with the philosophical systems of the Greeks.[24]

(1950), 40-58 and E.D.Rawson, *Intellectual Life in the Late Roman Republic* (forthcoming). Note also the popular account (based on the experiences of Cicero and his son) in S.F.Bonner, *Education in Ancient Rome* (London, 1977), 90-96. For Polybius' stay in Rome, see Astin, *Scipio*, 3-4, 14-20 and, more generally, F.W.Walbank, *Polybius* (Berkeley, 1972), 1-31. Astin also discusses (pp.294-306) the relations of Panaetius with the Roman elite. A.D.Momigliano, *Alien Wisdom: the Limits of Hellenization* (Cambridge, 1975) offers an important treatment of the intellectual position of Polybius in relation to Roman society and history (pp.22-49). For Arcesilaus, see Bianchi Bandinelli, *Rome*, 48-49.
23. On Cicero's Sullan library, see Plutarch, *Life of Sulla*, 26, 1 and Cicero, *Letters to Atticus* 4, 10 (Shackleton Bailey 84), 1; and, in general, *Letters to Atticus* 1, 20 (Shackleton Bailey 20), 7; *Letters to his Friends* 13, 77 (Shackleton Bailey 212), 3 with A.J.Marshall, 'Library Resources and Creative Writing at Rome', *Phoenix* 30 (1976), 252-264.
24. For an introduction to the full range of Cicero's literary creativity (including the philosophy), see A.E.Douglas, *Cicero* (*Greece and Rome* New Survey 2, Oxford, 1968). For his philosophical works, in particular, see Rawson, *Cicero*, 230-247 (and for the analysis

A different use of Greek philosophy is shown by the philosophical poem of Lucretius (94-55), *De Rerum Natura* (*On the Nature of Things*). Rather than integrating the Roman with the Greek, this Epicurean poem implicitly and explicitly attacks some of the most traditional Roman religious and cultural attitudes. This raises the problem of what we may call counter-culture.[25]

By the late second century, literature was used at Rome to attack traditional aristocratic values and to present a positive alternative. This was a result of the tremendous cultural take-off—whose impetus was such that it could not any longer be delimited by the needs of the governing class—and also of the growing number of independent writers. Lucilius provides an early example of this phenomenon; for his Satires include jests against various aspects of Roman social life and attacks on members of the elite. An even more striking example than the poetry of Lucretius are the verses of Catullus; he not only attacked prominent aristocrats in his epigrams, but also in his love poetry subverted traditional Roman notions of marriage and, in Poem 64 (which follows many of the conventions of Hellenistic epic poetry) challenged expectations by linking the love story of Theseus and Ariadne with a presentation of Achilles as brutal murderer rather than as epic hero.[26]

Our picture of literary activity in Rome and Italy in the first century is thus one of activity over an enormous range, accessible in common to writer and reader alike. The pattern in Roman art in the first century is similar, as artists and patrons explored the entire gamut of stylistic choices, from archaic through classical to Hellenistic, which were on offer from the Greek world. A striking, and indeed Roman, feature of the art of the period is the blending of different styles in a single work of art. The result sometimes seems grotesque to those

---

a portrait (London, 1975), 230-247 (and for the analysis of one major work, E.D.Rawson, 'The Interpretation of Cicero's *De Legibus*', *ANRW* 1, 4 (1973), 334-356). Note also the difficult, but important, article by E.D.Rawson—'The Introduction of Logical Organisation in Roman Prose Literature', *PBSR* 33 (1978), 12-34.

25. For Lucretius, see B.Farrington, 'Form and Purpose in the *De Rerum Natura*', in D.R.Dudley (ed.), *Lucretius* (London, 1965), 19-34; and, stressing the aspect of counter-culture, B.Farrington, *Science and Politics in the Ancient World* (London, 1939) is still useful. A good introduction is provided by E.J.Kenney, *Lucretius* (Greece and Rome New Survey 11, Oxford, 1977).

26. For the 'barbs' of Lucilius, see M.Coffey, *Roman Satire* (London and New York, 1976), 47-52. The subversion of traditional norms of marriage in the poetry of Catullus is well discussed by R.O.A.M.Lyne, *The Latin Love Poets* (Oxford, 1980), 1-61; and for Catullus' use of the 'epyllion' ('a little epic'), see L.C.Curran, 'Catullus 64 and the Heroic Age', *YClS* 21 (1969), 171-192; J.C.Bramble, 'Structure and Ambiguity in Catullus 64', *PCPhS* 16 (1970), 22-41.

familiar with Greek art, but this phenomenon should be seen primarily in terms of the exuberant open-mindedness of the artistic culture of the late Republic.[27]

If we look forward to the reign of Augustus, we see a tendency to greater uniformity and conformity, not only in the field of artistic production, but also in literature, as men turned more and more to the classical models of fifth- and fourth-century Greece. But another aspect of the culture of the reign of Augustus is perhaps more important. As we have seen, the late Republic had witnessed the development of an elite culture drawing on both Greek and Roman traditions; this development was crucial to the functioning of the relatively complex structure of the Roman Empire. For the shared culture and values of the governing class not only served to identify it, but also provided it with a political and moral language which enabled it to govern.[28]

---

27. Note the remarks of A.Stewart, *Attika: studies in Athenian sculpture of the Hellenistic age* (Hellenic Society Supplement 14, London, 1979), 142-148, with the comments of Smith, 'Portraiture'.

28. For a clear introduction to Augustan art see Walker and Burnett, *Image of Augustus*. On the classicizing culture of the Augustan period in general, see E.Gabba, 'The Historians and Augustus' in F.G.B.Millar and E.Segal (edd.), *Caesar Augustus:seven aspects* (Oxford, 1984), 61-88. The relationship between Augustus and leading Greek intellectuals is discussed by G.W.Bowersock, *Augustus and the Greek World* (Oxford, 1965), 30-41 (and for the development of a Graeco-Roman literary tradition, see pp. 122-139).

Chapter Three

RELIGION

'Roman religion' is a vast category, comprising many different elements. If we were transported back to the city of Rome in the first
century BC—or to the towns and countryside of Italy and Rome's
empire—we would find an enormous range of practices, institutions
and beliefs that we would call 'religious'. In private houses we would
find small shrines dedicated to the gods of the household; in the country, remote sanctuaries to local deities tended by the scattered inhabitants round about; in towns, imposing temples—not, like our churches,
centres of worship, but the earthly residences of the gods, present in
the form of costly statues. We would notice farmers killing animals
in sacrifice to the gods before sowing their crops or harvesting; the
sick appealing to the gods of healing; the aggrieved calling down divine
punishment in curses upon their enemies. We would observe public
festivals in which whole towns joined in celebrating their patron deity;
or private family rituals of burial and cremation. All these, and much
more, were parts of Roman religion.[1]

In this section we shall consider just one element of the whole: the
traditional 'official' religion of the city of Rome. This choice is justified for two principal reasons. First, it is the only area of Roman religion
whose characteristics we can delineate in some detail. In all other
cases—in, for example, the private cults of the household or the public rituals of the smaller towns of Italy—the surviving literary and
archaeological evidence allows us to say little more than 'they happened'.[2] Secondly, we firmly believe (though we cannot finally prove)

1. There is no reliable modern handbook of Roman religion in English. The best
introduction (though primarily concerned with the period of the early principate) is
J. Ward-Perkins and A. Claridge, *Pompeii AD 79* (Royal Academy of Arts Exhibition
Catalogue, Bristol, 1976), 55-61. Other useful guides are: Ogilvie, *Romans and their Gods*;
Scullard, *Festivals*; Warde-Fowler, *The Religious Experience*. Dumézil, *Archaic Roman Religion*,
is of fundamental importance, though much more specialized.
2. A simple account of Roman private religion is given by Ogilvie, *Romans and their
Gods*, 100-105. Archaeological evidence for household cults is laid out in G.K.Boyce,
Corpus of the Lararia of Pompeii, *MAAR* 14 (1937), while the private rituals associated

that this 'official' Roman state cult was the crucial defining element of the religious system as a whole. Here was to be found the 'Romanness' of Roman religion; here was the centre around which other elements took a secondary place. It thus deserves special attention.

Understanding religion

One major obstacle to a full understanding of Roman religion lies in our own preconceptions of the characteristics and functions of religious systems in general. For it is hard for anyone born into our society (whether a Christian or not) to distance themselves from a complex set of essentially Judaeo-Christian assumptions as to what a religion is supposed to be and do: that, for example, it should influence a man's private morality; that a religion should involve a personal relationship between believer and God; that private acts of prayer and devotion are of great importance in the observance of a religion; and so on. It is correspondingly hard to avoid using these assumptions as criteria for judging the 'quality' of Roman religion and for assessing the significance of particular changes within it. To some extent this is inevitable and accceptable. We can never rid ourselves entirely of our preconceptions and write neutral, objective history; nor would we want to. But the real problem with our religious attitudes is not so much that they are simply preconceptions, but that we fail to recognise them as such. We treat them as universal and objective facts and use them as if they provided a neutral framework for assessing Roman religion: private acts of devotion were rare in the Republic—therefore religion was failing to fulfil its 'proper' function; religious means were used to gain political ends—therefore 'true' Roman religion had been perverted away from its proper use. In fact, of course, different religions work in different ways and our normal framework is neither objective nor neutral. It is a blinkered judgment on foreign customs and practices, made according to our own specific cultural rules.[3]

---

with death are discussed by J.M.C.Toynbee, *Death and Burial in the Roman World* (London, 1971), 43-64. For a clear treatment of the surviving material from an Italian shrine, see *Mysteries of Diana: the Antiquities from Nemi in Nottingham Museums* (Castle Museum, Nottingham, 1983). Lavish illustrations of votive offerings from such shrines are provided by P.Pensabene et al. *Terracotte votive dal Tevere* (Studi Miscellanei 25, Rome, 1980) and L.Gatti lo Guzzo, *Il deposito votivo dall' Esquilino detto di Minerva Medica* (Studi e materiali di etruscologia e antichità Italiche 17, Rome, 1978).
3. For theoretical discussions of religion in a cross-cultural perspective, see E.E.Evans-Pritchard, *Theories of Primitive Religion* (Oxford, 1965) and, more technically, Banton, *Anthropological Approaches*. Evocative accounts of two very different religious systems are

An analogy drawn from an area nearer home may make this point clearer. Consider the reaction of an unintelligent fan of English Soccer who finds himself, by chance, at an American Football match. He recognises that the game falls broadly into the category with which he is familiar (teams getting a ball into some defined spot on a large grass pitch)—and then complains that the referee is failing in his job by letting the men handle the ball and hit each other. In response to this we would all agree that the man would get nothing out of the game until he overcame his mad assumption that all football was English Football and made some effort to learn the American game. The problem is similar for us in studying Roman religion—we will get nowhere unless we try to escape from our Christianizing assumptions of how a religion *should* be, and discover the specific rules appropriate to the religion of Rome.[4]

This section then will lay great stress on the constant unchanging elements of the Roman religious system. Drawing principally on the plentiful literary evidence of the first century, it will attempt to highlight the underlying rules specific to that religion. In second place it will consider the ways in which the religion of the final phase of the Republic differed from that of earlier periods.

The traditional view

This method of approach is very different from that usually adopted by historians dealing with Roman religion in the late Republic. In fact (despite a few recent and refreshing exceptions) most treatments of this subject present a view radically opposed to ours. A summary of this traditional view may be helpful, given its prominence in many histories of the period.[5]

---

given by E.E.Evans-Pritchard, *Nuer Religion* (Oxford, 1956) and D.K.Jordan, *Gods, Ghosts and Ancestors: the Folk Religion of a Taiwanese Village* (Berkeley, 1972).
4. For a sophisticated discussion of the intelligibility of other cultures' religions, see two essays in B.R.Wilson (ed.), *Rationality* (Oxford, 1970): P. Winch, 'Understanding a Primitive Society' (pp.78-111) and A.MacIntyre, 'The Idea of a Social Science' (pp.112-130).
5. An extreme statement of this traditional view is given by Taylor, *Party Politics*, 76-97. Note also A.D.Nock in *Cambridge Ancient History*, 10 , 465-471 and Warde-Fowler, *The Religious Experience*, esp. 303-307; 335-356; 357-358; 428-451. Exceptions to this standard view are, principally, the following: H.D.Jocelyn, 'The Roman Nobility and the Religion of the Roman State', *Journal of Religious History* 4 (1966), 89-104; North, 'Conservatism and Change'; Liebeschuetz, *Continuity and Change*, esp. 1-100; Wardman, *Religion and Statecraft*, esp. 1-79.

Its central thesis is that the religion of the late Republic was in decline—either neglected or merely manipulated as a useful weapon in the political battles of the governing elite. The start of this decline is normally dated to the late third century BC and is related to two principal causes: the fundamental inadequacies of Roman paganism and the growing influence in Rome of Greek ideas. These together led to the growth of scepticism among the governing class (through their contact with the irreligious notions of Greek philosophy) and to an influx of Eastern cults, which catered for the emotional needs not satisfied by the dry formalistic state religion, and yet in turn served to pollute that religion with foreign elements.

A variety of evidence is adduced to support this view. Proof of the manipulation of religion is found in the use (or misuse) of omens and oracles in political life—and especially in those instances where a political leader seems to have invented an oracular response to support his own position, or pretended to have spotted an adverse omen, which might necessitate (according to religious law) the cancellation of an assembly. Neglect seems similarly easy to substantiate. It is certainly the case, for example, that by the first century BC several ancient religious rituals were no longer carried out; while the emperor Augustus' claim to have restored 82 temples seems to suggest that these buildings had been ill-cared for in the immediately preceding period—that is the late Republic.[6]

We disagree fundamentally with this characterization of late Republican religion. It will be obvious from our brief presentation that it is founded on a range of Christianizing assumptions similar to those we have already criticized: the erroneous view that a religion must cater for the *emotional needs* of its consumers; the belief that politics and religion ought not to be intertwined. Without embarking here on a full deconstruction of the argument, we wish to highlight some additional problems of approach and interpretation.

The first difficulty lies in the neglect of religion. In some cases this is inadequately proven: we do not need to conclude, for example, from Augustus' boastful claims that the temples of Rome were widely dilapidated, beyond the consequences of normal wear and tear; nor is such

6. The 'invention' of a Sibylline oracle in 56 BC is often cited in this context. For the background, see Stockton, *Cicero*, 197-204. The contemporary letters of Cicero clearly state that the oracle in question was a forgery; see *Letters to his Friends* 1, 1 (Shackleton Bailey 12), 1; 1, 4 (Shackleton Bailey 14), 2. Note also the supposedly fraudulent declaration of a bad omen by Pompey—Plutarch, *Life of Cato the Younger* 42. For Augustus' restoration of temples and his revival of archaic ritual, see *Res Gestae Divi Augusti* (*The Achievements of the Divine Augustus*), 20 and Suetonius, *Life of Augustus* 31, 4.

dilapidation confirmed by contemporary late Republican evidence.[7] In other cases the problem lies not with the 'facts' of neglect, but with the interpretation placed on them. Consider the disappearance of that ritual in which the priests called *fetiales* formally initiated war by travelling to the borders of enemy territory and casting their spears into it. Does this necessarily indicate, as the traditional view has it, a decline in religious observance? Does it not rather suggest that the religion of the state, by discarding certain elements, was adapting to changing circumstances? In this instance a ritual which had originated when Rome was fighting hostile neighbours in the peninsula of Italy could no longer seem appropriate when her wars were fought overseas, hundreds of miles away.[8]

So too with importation and innovation. This is best seen as a positive means of growth and adaptation, not as some desperate remedy for the inadequacy of native cult. Roman religion had borrowed from the outside from as far back as we can trace it. Indeed by the fifth century BC, Apollo, as well as Castor and Pollux, had already been imported from Greece. This openness and flexibility was simply a characteristic of Roman religion—just as openness to new citizens was (as we shall see, p. 78) a characteristic of Roman political organisation. It was certainly not a clear indication of Roman religious failure.[9]

The problem of manipulation is also too crudely handled by the traditional view. Many features of many religions seem odd—or even fraudulent—from the outside. Modern Catholicism in south Italy, for example, gives an important place to many miracles that we regard as utterly spurious. Yet, as a religion, it undoubtedly flourishes. We should not assume that because, say, some Roman oracles seem to us

---

7. We should remember that floods, fire and storms had always been a danger to the temples. The late Republic fared no better or worse in this respect. See, Wardman, *Religion and Statecraft*, 70-71. For late Republican restoration of temples, see Cicero, *Letters to his Brother Quintus* 3,1 (Shackleton Bailey 21), 14 (Cicero's restoration of the Temple of Tellus) and *Against Verres*(2) 1, 49, 129—60, 154 (Verres' restoration of the Temple of Castor, no doubt unfairly criticized by Cicero in the interests of his case).
8. On the history of the Fetial procedure, see Harris, *War and Imperialism*, 166-175. For the role of the Fetials in treaty-making and the suggestion of its revival in the second century, see E.D.Rawson, 'Scipio, Laelius, Furius and the Ancestral Religion', *JRS* 63 (1973) esp.166-168.
9. See North, 'Conservatism and Change'. For a sophisticated discussion of religious changes, dealing with a slighty later period, see R.L.Gordon, 'Mithraism and Roman Society: Social Factors in the Explanation of Religious Change', *Religion* 2, 2 (1972), 92-121. Early imports into the Roman religious system are discussed by Dumézil, *Archaic Roman Religion*, 441-445 and S.Weinstock, 'Two Archaic Inscriptions from Latium', *JRS* 50 (1960), 112-114 (on Castor and Pollux).

fraudulent, the whole religious system was failing. So-called 'manipu-lation' can only be properly assessed by setting it in the context of the specific attitudes and rules of the religious system concerned.[10]

An alternative approach

Our own, very different, view of the operation of the Roman religious system lays greatest stress on an understanding of those rules. There are three main points.

1. The first is that the religion of Republican Rome was essentially a public religion. In contrast to the modern Western stress on private manifestations of religious commitment, religious observance in Rome consisted primarily in public or communal rituals and the interests of the gods were perceived to lie above all in the business of state, in political and military action.

A clear illustration of this point is found in the character of the Roman priesthood. Official priests in Rome were quite unlike most priests in the modern world. They were not specially trained 'profes-sionals'; they had no particular pastoral responsibilities in the city; they did not devote a large proportion of their life to the duties of their priest-hood. So, for example, no Roman would have gone to a priest, in par-ticular, for advice on moral problems or for teaching in religious dogma. Roman priests were merely a sub-group of the Roman political elite, who acted as expert advisers on religious matters and carried out or supervised particular rituals and sacrifices. The same men, by and large, filled the roles of leading politicians and state priests. This was no accident, no failure on the part of the Romans to differentiate ade-quately between different specific functions. It was a natural corollary of a religious system that was embedded in the political—or a politi-cal system embedded in the religious.[11]

---

10. For a theoretical perspective on the 'manipulation' of religion, see the remarks of M.Spiro ('Religion: Problems of Definition and Explanation') in Banton, *Anthropologi-cal Approaches*, 105-106. See also E.E.Evans-Pritchard, *Witchcraft, Oracles and Magic among the Azande* (Oxford, 1976) for examples of (to us) clear 'manipulation' of religion, not perceived as such by the practitioners concerned.
11. For a brief discussion of the duties of the various Roman priests, see Scullard, *Fes-tivals*, 27-31 or Wardman, *Religion and Statecraft*, 16-21. G.Szemler, *The Priests of the Roman Republic* (Coll. Lat., 127, Brussels, 1972), 21-46 usefully summarizes important Ger-man work on the functions of Roman priests. See also, Cicero, *On his House* (esp. 1, 1-3), a speech delivered before the college of *pontifices*. Most modern discussions of Roman priesthood have been concerned with the place of priesthood within a man's political career and with the political role of the priestly colleges; see, for example,

Another indication of the public bias of Roman religion is found in the exclamations to the gods (*o di, per deos immortales* etc.) made by Cicero in his private letters. Although these are highly conventional- ized expressions, employed without much conscious thought, they nevertheless display in their usage a clear pattern: in very nearly every case Cicero's appeals to the divine occur in the context of political or military events (the conduct of a consul or business in the senate) and not in the context of his personal life and emotions. The gods were naturally associated not with private, but with public areas of life.[12]

2. The second major point is concerned with the precise character of this divine involvement in Roman politics and war: that is, the interest of the gods always lay in promoting the success of the Roman state and they took a direct part (either independently or in cooperation with men) in bringing about that end. They were not passive deities whose interests lay in moral values beyond the concerns of day to day politics.[13]

The consequences of this apparently simple characterization are important for understanding many aspects of political argument and action in the late Republic. In some cases the consequences are obvi- ous. It is, for example, well recognised that the Roman idea of a 'just war'—fought with the direct support of the gods and under the protec- tion of religious ritual—was not simply cynically invented to provide some justification for Roman military aggression. There was no need for cynicism. The Romans saw the interests of their state as served by military victory—and those interests were necessarily upheld by the gods. Divine support combined with the prowess of the soldiers to increase the power of Rome. It was axiomatic that the gods should be involved and approve.[14]

D.E.Hahm, 'Roman Nobility and the Three Major Priesthoods, 218-167 BC', *TAPhA* 94 (1963), 73-85; L.R.Taylor, 'Caesar's Colleagues in the Pontifical College', *AJPh* 63 (1942), 385-412.
12. For example, Cicero, *Letters to Atticus* 1, 18 (Shackleton Bailey 18), 5—an exclama- tion over the laziness of the consul, Afranius; *Letters to his Brother Quintus* 3, 2 (Shackle- ton Bailey 22) 2—an exclamation over attacks on Gabinius (consul 58) in the senate. Note that Cicero never appeals to the gods (*di*) in his anguish over the death of his daughter Tullia.
13. See, briefly, Wardman, *Religion and Statecraft*, 1-10; but note the interesting (though ultimately unconvincing) attempt by Liebeschuetz (*Continuity and Change*, 39-54) to argue for the particular concern of Roman deities with morality.
14. On the 'just war', see Brunt, 'Laus Imperii', in P.D.A.Garnsey and C.R.Whittaker (edd.), *Imperialism in the Ancient World* (Cambridge, 1979), esp. 175-178 and Harris, *War and Imperialism*, 166-175.

Other consequences are less immediately obvious. The most important of these is the opposition perceived by the Romans between, on the one hand, political leaders whose policies were beneficial for the state and who worked in cooperation with the gods and, on the other, their opponents who were necessarily out of harmony with the gods. Consider this for a moment from the point of view of Cicero. Believing that his policies were the best ones for Rome, he would automatically regard himself as supporting (and supported by) the interests of the gods. Indeed on several occasions, in both his public speeches and private correspondence, he claims explicitly that he enjoyed direct divine assistance in carrying out his policies. It would naturally follow for Cicero that his political opponents—Catiline, Clodius and the rest, whose activities were (to his mind) bringing ruin on the state—were in a relationship not of cooperation, but of enmity with the gods. Of course, these men no doubt saw things rather differently, linking themselves, not Cicero, to the cause of the gods. But the basic opposition between divine favour and disfavour remained.[15]

This opposition illuminates one striking aspect of Roman political rhetoric. In his speeches, Cicero often designates his adversary 'the enemy of the gods' and credits him with actions that confirm such a designation. The opponent is, for example, said to have destroyed religious shrines, polluted divine festivals or neglected sacred rituals—in contrast to the properly pious behaviour of Cicero and his clients. Modern scholars have tended to treat this theme as simply one of the 'conventions' of rhetoric and offer little further explanation. Yet do commonplaces of this type become 'conventions' by chance? Surely they are 'conventional' precisely because they are founded upon society's most firmly held values. Far from being *merely* a literary device, Cicero's rhetoric about his opponent's enmity of the gods gained its force from the ideological principle we have outlined: that the good politician enjoyed divine support, while his adversary was necessarily in a relationship of hostility with the gods.[16]

This principle also helps us to understand those incidents (often

---

15. For Cicero's claim to have enjoyed direct aid from the gods in the suppression of Catiline, see *Letters to Atticus* 1, 16 (Shackleton Bailey 16), 6 and *Against Catiline* 2, 13, 29.
16. The theme of 'the enemy of the gods' appears in (for example) Cicero's *Philippics* 1, 10, 25; 3, 4, 9; 5, 3, 7 (referring to Mark Antony) and *Against Catiline* 1, 5, 12; 4, 11, 24. Such expressions are treated largely as rhetorical commonplaces by R.J.Goar, *Cicero and the State Religion* (Amsterdam, 1972), 36-45 and U.M.Heibges, 'Religion and Rhetoric in Cicero's Speeches', *Latomus* 28 (1969), 833-849; although both authors recognise that some religious feeling must have been left in Cicero's audience for such devices to have had any effect. For a clear account on the relation of language and ideology, see C. Belsey, *Critical Practice* (London, 1980), 42-46.

dismissed as fraud) in which assemblies were cancelled or interrupted by the declaration of bad omens. The first important point here is that in Rome all formal political activity took place in an explicitly religious context. Assemblies were preceded by religious ritual to ascertain that the gods approved their being held, and magistrates, when conducting political business with the people, always had to occupy specifically religious ground: that is, they stood in a *templum*, not necessarily a 'temple' in our sense, but any specially consecrated area, such as the platform for speakers in the Forum.[17]

In this religious context, the principle of opposition between those politicians with divine support and those in a position of enmity with the gods once again operated—as the logic underlying the religious hindrance of assemblies. A purely hypothetical example will make this clear. Imagine Cicero again. Suppose he had just learnt that an assembly was to be convened by one of his arch-enemies, with the aim of introducing legislation that was, to his mind, misguided or even dangerous. It would appear to him axiomatic that the gods also disapproved of the proposals and would regard any assembly convened to enact such legislation as in conflict with their will. The proper links between the gods and political activity were thus ruptured; and it would seem inevitable to Cicero that divine disapproval would be displayed and ill omens be sighted. The holding of the assembly was already, in religious terms, incorrect.

Did Roman politicians consciously rehearse this reasoning when they held up proceedings of the assembly by declaring a bad omen? We cannot know. But it is misleading and ethnocentric of us to put it all down to a combination of clever fraud by the declarer and simpleminded acceptance by the assembly. It is easy to be sceptical about other people's religions. The important point is that religious hindrance (dishonest or not) can be seen to make some consistent sense in the context of the Roman religious rules. It had an underlying logic—as we have laid out step by step—and only because of this did it work; and only through this can it properly be understood.[18]

---

17. For the religious context of assemblies, see Staveley, *Voting*, 149-52. The notion of *templum* is most clearly explained by W.Smith etc, *A Dictionary of Greek and Roman Antiquities* vol. 2 (London, 1891), 772-773. See also Livy, *History of Rome* 1, 18, 6-10 and A.L.Frothingham, 'Ancient Orientation Unveiled, II, Etruria and Rome', *AJA* 21 (1917), 187-201.
18. Consider, for example, the incident of 57 BC when Milo obstructed an election by announcing evil omens to the presiding magistrate; Cicero, *Letters to Atticus* 4, 3 (Shackleton Bailey 75), 3-4. Although normally treated as an entirely 'political' incident (by, eg, Stockton, *Cicero*, 202; Gruen, *Last Generation*, 294-298), it can only be fully understood if it is seen also in a religious context.

3. Our third main point concerns the focus of communication between men and gods. In the modern Christian church the priest dispenses Communion wine and bread to the congregation, and so, in some sense, acts as an intermediary between them and God. We might be tempted to assume that priests in Rome filled a similar role. In fact they did not.

In Rome this mediating role was filled by men we usually think of in strictly political terms. On the one hand, the magistrates had important religious functions;[19] but beyond these, the senate provided the principal link between men and gods and controlled men's behaviour towards the gods. Priests (as we have already indicated, p. 30) provided specialist advice in religious matters—but they lacked authoritative power in that area. Clearest evidence for this is found in the handling of religious problems, such as the incident in 62, when Clodius (tribune 58) sacrilegiously infiltrated the annual festival of the Good Goddess, traditionally open to married women only. Priests, as usual, gave their specialist opinions, but the final decision rested with the senate. Similarly with prodigies—strange events, such as showers of blood from the sky or androgynous births, generally reckoned to be signs of divine anger, requiring rites of expiation. It was the senate that decided which of the many such events reported really did have religious significance.[20]

An important negative indication also confirms the central position of the senate in the religious system of the state. Unlike the assemblies, its business was never (as far as we know) interrupted by the kind of religious obstruction, through adverse omens, that sometimes affected the business of assemblies. This fact seems strange, since senatorial meetings were politically just as significant as those of assemblies. It is best explained by reference to the special religious position of the senate. Unlike assemblies (which could on occasion be deemed to be in an improper relationship to the gods), the senate, as

---

19. For this mediating function of magistrates, note their role in 'taking the auspices' before assemblies (Greenidge, *Roman Public Life*, 36-40, 162-167) and the ceremony at which the consuls 'took the auspices' at the beginning of their year of office (Scullard, *Festivals*, 52-53).

20. A straightforward account of the Bona Dea ceremonies is given by Scullard, *Festivals*, 199-201. The role of the senate is brought out clearly by Cicero, *Letters to Atticus* 1, 13 (Shackleton Bailey 13), 3 and J.P.V.D.Balsdon, 'Fabula Clodiana', *Historia* 15 (1966), 65-73 (though it is a very 'political' account). For further discussion, see Wiseman, *Cinna the Poet*, 130-137. The procedure for handling prodigies is clearly described by Livy, *History of Rome* 22, 1, 8-20; 40, 19, 1-5. Note also the detailed monograph of B.Mac-Bain, *Prodigy and Expiation: a Study in Religion and Politics in Republican Rome* (Coll.Lat.177, Brussels, 1982).

direct focus of communication between gods and men, could never be out of harmony with the divine. So, logically, its business could never be subject to interruption on religious grounds.[21]

We have discussed three major elements in the network of religious rules in Republican Rome: the focus of divine interest; the character of divine involvement in Roman politics and the relationship of the gods to political leaders; the human centre of mediation between gods and men. These provide some basis for constructing a picture of Roman religion in the late Republic very different from the traditional one. Briefly now we wish to raise three additional factors to sharpen the focus of that picture.

The first point is an admission of over-simplification. So far we have used the terms religion and politics as though they were separate categories; as though Roman usage broadly coincided with our own, subject only to such marginal differences as we have outlined—Roman religion, for example, was more concerned with politics than modern Christianity. This is a useful preliminary tactic. It makes telling the story easier. The real problem, however, is that in the Roman world those two categories did not exist as distinct entities, but were inextricably intertwined. Indeed there is no exact equivalent in Latin of our words 'religion' and 'politics'. Any full account of Roman republican religion would need to go beyond our brief summary, to highlight in its analysis this fundamental difference between Roman ideas and our own.[22]

The second point returns to the varieties of Roman religious experience we evoked at the very beginning of this section—and particularly to private and domestic aspects of religion. We have so far justified our stress on the 'official' cult of the city of Rome by suggesting that it provided the central focus and defining characteristics of the Roman religious system as a whole. But the historian cannot entirely ignore other types of religious practice. Despite the general lack of evidence, we wish to make one important (negative) observation on the significance of private and family cults. It has sometimes been claimed that these offered the Romans a kind of personal satisfaction entirely lacking in public religion. There is no justification for that view. Although proof is impossible, we firmly believe that the vast

21. The absence of religious obstruction in the senate is also pointed out by Liebeschuetz, *Continuity and Change*, 15.
22. For the sense of *religio* and the adjective *religiosus*, see Cicero, *On the Nature of the Gods* 2, 28, 72; Aulus Gellius, *Attic Nights* 4, 9. Note also the discussion of Dumézil, *Archaic Roman Religion*, 129-133 and Wagenvoort, 'Characteristic Traits of Ancient Roman Religion', in *Pietas*, 225-227.

majority of such cults essentially represented the state cult on a smaller scale—practised within the smaller social unit of the family. To some individuals they may have been important, to others not; one cannot know. We would guess, however—and it must remain a guess—that detailed knowledge of these cults would not substantially alter our view of the distinguishing features of 'Roman religion'.[23]

The third issue is that of continuity. We have supported our view of the basic characteristics of Roman Republican religion with evidence drawn almost exclusively from the first century. That is where most of the evidence is. Did religion of the earlier periods of the Republic operate according to broadly similar rules? We cannot be certain; but we can reasonably *assume* that the central features of the religious system we have identified had long been present. It is surely impossible to conceive that all we know of the first century, with its complex religious/political configuration, was simply an invention of that period. Indeed such evidence as we have from earlier periods (writing of the second century, linguistic usage, deductions about the rituals and institutions of the preceding centuries) seems compatible with the broad picture we have outlined.[24]

Late Republican developments

This is not to deny any changes whatsoever in the religion of the late Republic. It is inconceivable that, in a time of such rapid changes in other areas, religion should have stood still. Let us now fill out our picture of the underlying principles of Republican religion by discussing briefly some of the developments characteristic of the second and first centuries. This discussion is necessarily limited by our inadequate knowledge of the religion of earlier periods, against which we might assess the changes.

Many of the developments in the late Republic may be understood as the necessary adaptations of religion to changing political and social circumstances. We have already mentioned the negative side of this,

---

23. Primary importance is given to private, family cults by, for example, Scullard, *Festivals*, 17 and Wagenvoort, 'Orare, Precari', *Pietas*, 203-206. Though starting from a different point of view from ours, Ogilvie, *Romans and their Gods*, 105 also comes to the conclusion that 'private worship was a miniature of public worship'.

24. A clear demonstration of the continuity in Roman religion from even the sixth century BC is given by Dumézil, *Archaic Roman Religion*, 83-88. The traditional connection of the gods and Roman success in war is traced back at least to the third century BC by Harris, *War and Imperialism*, 118-125. This connection is also demonstrated by the ancient ceremony of the *triumph*, in which the triumphing general was adorned in the garb of Jupiter Optimus Maximus; see H.Versnel, *Triumphus* (Leiden, 1979), 56-93.

pointing out that, as the Roman world expanded, the traditional ritual for the declaration of war died out. But the growth of empire brought also positive effects; new elements entered the religious system both inside and outside the city of Rome. An obvious example of this is the goddess Roma—a personalized representation of the Roman state—promoted by Rome for worship in her eastern conquests from the third century onwards. It is tempting to be cynical about what seems to be the mere invention of a new deity; but again a more sensitive approach is possible. As Roman political power extended, some means had to be found (whether consciously invented or not) of extending also the religious aspects of that power. The promotion of the goddess Roma in the East introduced into the expanding empire a visible symbol of the religious/political configuration we have been discussing.[25]

Adaptation also came with the changing character of political competition in the city. Religion, as we have stressed, was inextricably bound up with the political system. As the political system came increasingly under the dominance of powerful individuals, so those individuals tended also to monopolize links with divine. We shall see in the final section of this book that Julius Caesar monopolized those links to the extent of becoming (to all intents and purposes) a god himself. But this development had earlier roots. Publius Scipio Africanus, for example, who brought about the final defeat of Hannibal at the end of the third century, claimed a privileged relationship with Jupiter and was said to commune with the god privately in his temple on the Capitol. Sulla, dictator of the city in the 80s, boasted of special protection by the goddess Venus. This was a feature not simply of clever propaganda by these men, but of the tradition of cooperation and unity between politicians and the gods.[26]

The increasing violence and disorder of political life likewise had an effect on religion. For confusion easily arose where traditional religious practice was confronted with quite unprecedented political circumstances. The events of 59 illustrate this clearly. Julius Caesar, as consul, introduced a wide range of legislation, which was opposed by his colleague in the consulship, Marcus Bibulus. Bibulus, predictably,

---

25. See R.Mellor, *Thea Rome: the Worship of the Goddess Roma in the Greek World* (Hypomnemata 42, Göttingen, 1975).
26. On Scipio, see the introductory account in H.H.Scullard, *Scipio Africanus: Soldier and Politician* (London, 1970), 20-23 and the full review of the evidence by F.W.Walbank, 'The Scipionic Legend', *PCPhS* 13 (1967), 54-69. On Sulla's relations with Venus, see Plutarch, *Life of Sulla* 19; Appian, *The Civil Wars* 1, 97. J.P.V.D.Balsdon, 'Sulla Felix', *JRS* 41 (1951), 1-10 is not convincing in his suggestion that Sulla's connection was with the Greek Aphrodite rather than the Roman Venus.

intended to offer religious objection to those assemblies convened to pass this legislation. However, in the terrible disorder of that year he was unable to go out of his house for fear of the violence that would confront him. Accordingly he sent messages out, stating that he was looking for omens. This raised a problem. It seems to have been a requirement of objections of this type (called in Latin, *obnuntiatio*) that the bad omens should be announced personally, before the start of the assembly in question. Bibulus could not fulfil that requirement without risk to his life. Did his messages then constitute a proper religious objection? The situation had never arisen and it was not clear what the answer was. Caesar passed his legislation, but it was for a long time of doubtful status, subject to attack on the grounds that it had been passed against religious law. Incidents of this type have often been adduced as proof of decline of religion. In our view they indicate rather that religion continued to be important, though disrupted along with the normal political processes of the city.[27]

The two final developments we wish to discuss relate to the influence on Roman religion from the Greek world in the late Republic. While rejecting the view that Greek influence was one of the major causes of the decline of Roman religion, we would not wish to deny that Rome's growing links with Greece had important effects. First, contact with cults whose origin lay in the Eastern Mediterranean encouraged in Rome for the first time the development of groups whose sole purpose was religious. So far we have stressed that religion was embedded within the political system. Broadly speaking that is true— but from the second century on new kinds of 'religious' organizations did start to emerge in parallel (and not always in conflict) with traditional state cult. The most famous incident concerning these groups was the suppression by the senate in 186 BC of cults of Bacchus (the Greek Dionysus) in Italy; though that kind of persecution was not typical of Roman reactions. More often new cults were easily tolerated. From our point of view what is important about this development is that new kinds of religious *choices* were being offered to the Romans.

---

27. For the sanest account of this incident (broadly along the same lines as ours), see Lintott, *Violence*, 143-147; and, more technically, J.Linderski, 'Constitutional Aspects of the Consular Elections in 59 BC', *Historia* 14 (1965), 423-442. Most discussions of Bibulus' actions assume that he was correctly 'obnuntiating' and consider the incident in the context of the laws regulating *obnuntiatio* and the supposed repeal of those laws by Clodius. See, for example, A.E.Astin, 'Leges Aelia et Fufia', *Latomus* 23 (1964), 421-445 and J.P.V.D.Balsdon, 'Roman History 58-56 BC: Three Ciceronian Problems', *JRS* 47 (1957), 15-16 (suggesting that Bibulus *abused* the practice of *obnuntiatio*).

The state cult in the end would become only one religious option among many.[28]

The last point relates to the issue of the importation of Hellenizing culture that we discussed in the previous section. Rome's eventual contact with the developed traditions of Greek philosophy led, by the very last period of the Republic, to the growth of an intellectual attitude towards the traditional cult. Cicero, for example, in his attempts to unite Greek theory with traditional Roman ways of thought (see p. 22) considered various important aspects of Roman state religion. One of his treatises dealt with the practice of divination and whether the gods did in fact allow men to know the future course of events. This was not the work of out-and-out scepticism that it is usually supposed to be; Cicero did not come to the firm conclusion that divination was impossible. Yet it was an innovation that Cicero could present, among other views, that sharply sceptical alternative. Religion was being exposed for the first time to self-conscious, intellectual scrutiny.[29]

28. Note especially the fundamental articles by J.A.North—'Religious Toleration in Republican Rome', *PCPhS* 25 (1979), 85-103 and 'Novelty and Choice in Roman Religion', *JRS* 70 (1980), 186-191. On religious tolerance in the ancient world more generally, see A.Momigliano, in S.C.Humphreys (ed.), *Anthropology and the Greeks* (London, 1978), 179-193. For a simple account of the introduction into Rome and Italy of one particular new cult, see R.E.Witt, *Isis in the Graeco-Roman World* (London, 1971), 70-88.
29. Cicero's *On Divination* is a dialogue in two books. In the first, arguments supporting the validity of the practice of divination (from a Stoic philosophical perspective) are put in the mouth of Cicero's brother Quintus. In the second, the character of Cicero himself takes a sceptical line and argues against the possibility that the gods foretell the future to men. Although some weight is given to the sceptical argument, as it is put into the mouth of Cicero himself, it should not necessarily be considered as the 'real views' of the author. In a related dialogue (*On the Nature of the Gods*) the character of Cicero explicitly approves (like Quintus in *On Divination*) of a Stoic view of theology. For the literary context of these dialogues, see above pp. 20-24.

Chapter Four

POLITICAL INSTITUTIONS

It is difficult to comprehend political life at Rome in the late Republic. Not only are its structures and institutions alien to us; they were also in a state of disruption and change. We have decided to treat this two-faceted problem in two parts: this chapter deals with the traditional, structural features of Roman politics; the next considers in greater detail the practice of political life in the final phase of the Republic—how the system worked and how it was disrupted. The division is, of course, schematic. Not everything fits neatly into one section or the other. Nevertheless we believe that it is a helpful way of dealing with a complex problem.

Status

From the top to the bottom—from the world of the most powerful senator to that of the humblest slave—Roman society was sharply stratified. Divisions of status underlay all social and political life: divisions between the free man and the slave; the citizen and the non-citizen; the senator and equestrian; the patrician and plebeian. This point deserves great emphasis. All Romans knew their place.[1]

Is this so surprising or distinctive? Twentieth-century western society, after all, still has its class structure; social position is still important. That is true—but the stratification of Roman society was of a quite different kind. Status divisions at Rome were more complex than our own, more precisely and legally defined, more closely linked to political rights, far more pervasive. Consider, for example, how often Cicero adds a rank to the names he quotes: Caius Mustius, a Roman knight...; Caius Pictus, a senator...; Publius Umbrenus, an ex-slave... This may seem to us gratuitous or redundant. It was not redundant

---

1. The importance of status is stressed by Crook, *Law and Life*, 36-67, which provides a clear account of the major status divisions at Rome.

in the Roman context. Personal status mattered.[2]

From all the complex layers of this stratified system, let us consider just one or two of its elements; this will prompt discussion of more general characteristics of the system as a whole.

First the axis of freedom and citizenship. Imagine the total population of the city of Rome in the 50s BC—almost a million people in all. It is easy to say that a proportion were slaves, the rest free; that some were citizens, some not. But it was, in fact, more complicated than that. The question 'Are you a Roman citizen?' might not have brought the straightforward yes/no answer we are tempted to suppose.[3]

The extremes of legal status are clear enough. At the top were about 200,000 male citizens, the sons of citizen parents. These enjoyed the protection of Roman law and political rights—that of voting and (for the few who had sufficient wealth) standing for office. At the bottom were the slaves—perhaps about 300,000 men, women and children—with no political or legal rights whatsoever. They were, in theory, as much the property of their master as his furniture.[4]

Between these extreme categories, however, were a variety of intermediate ranks—free persons, but not citizens in the fullest sense. Ex-slaves, for example, those formally freed by their masters, became Roman citizens, but with somewhat curtailed rights. They could vote, but neither serve in the legions (as freeborn citizens could) nor seek political office.[5] Women—the wives and daughters of citizens—were entirely excluded from political activity, with no vote nor right to undertake political office; yet they could be regarded as citizens to the extent that they came under the protection (or restriction) of Roman law.[6]

---

2. Note also, as Crook points out (*Law and Life*, 38), that Gaius, a lawyer of the second century AD, in writing an introduction to Roman law (*The Institutes*), devoted one book out of four—and that the first—to the law of status.

3. For the population of Rome, see (most clearly) Hopkins, *Conquerors and Slaves*, 96-98.

4. In addition to the section cited in note 1, see Crook, *Law and Life*, 179-191 (on slaves) and 255-259 (on citizens). Ancient evidence (in translation) on Roman slavery is collected by T.Wiedemann, *Greek and Roman Slavery* (London, 1981); for the slave as property, see pp.15-35. See also, M.I.Finley, *Ancient Slavery and Modern Ideology* (London, 1980) and M.I.Finley (ed.), *Slavery in Classical Antiquity* (Cambridge, 1960). For the slaves as workers and producers, see D.W.Rathbone, 'The Slave Mode of Production in Italy', *JRS* 73 (1983), 160-168. The role of the Roman citizen in political life is fully treated by Nicolet, *World of the Citizen*.

5. See Treggiari, *Freedmen* (especially pp.1-86, for the legal rights of freedmen).

6. Ancient evidence (in translation) on Roman women is collected by M.R.Lefkowitz and M.B.Fant, *Women's Life in Greece and Rome: a Source Book in Translation* (London, 1982), 131-282 (especially pp. 173-203 for the rights of women in law). The best general introduction to Roman women is S.B.Pomeroy, *Goddesses, Whores, Wives and Slaves* (London, 1976), 149-226. This modifies the classic statement of M.I.Finley ('The Silent Women of Rome',

In addition, outsiders of various types were resident in the city. Some of these—by the 50s most Italians—would have possessed full citizenship. Others would have had no *Roman* status at all, or only very limited rights.[7]

The complexity of these types of status was in part a consequence of Rome's generosity with her citizenship—not (as we might imagine) an indication of its jealous guarding of full citizen status. This contrasts sharply with other cities in the ancient world. The fifth-century Athenians, for example, did not grant to their ex-slaves any form of Athenian citizenship; nor did they start to incorporate the inhabitants of their empire into citizen status. Rome's policy of wide incorporation was unusual and led to the development of a range of categories of citizenship designed to cope with incoming outsiders.[8]

The status divisions between full Roman citizens themselves were even more complex. They held basic political and legal rights in common—and were thus distinguished, as a group, from outsiders; but they were not, even formally, equals.

The most striking aspect of their stratification is found in the so-called census 'classes'. On average every six years senior magistrates—censors—were appointed. Their main task was to conduct a registration of all citizens (*census*) and to divide them into hierarchical 'classes' according to the amount of wealth each possessed. There were five main grades (Latin: *classes*) in this hierarchy, with an additional elevated 'equestrian' category (which we shall discuss below) and an additional large bottom rank—*capite censi* (those enrolled by a head count)—which consisted of men whose property did not entitle them to a place in even the lowest grade. The original principle behind this division had lain in the military organization of the city: the wealthier grades, for example, were required to provide for themselves more expensive fighting equipment and, right up until Marius' levy in 107 BC (p. 7), the *capite censi* could not legally be enrolled in the army, except in emergencies. By the first century BC, however, that military function of the census was no longer of any consequence, and indeed the census as a whole was rarely completed in the disruption of the final years

---

in *Aspects of Antiquity* (London, 1968), 129-142) that even the aristocratic women of Rome in the late Republic filled a role of entire subservience, imposed upon them by their menfolk.

7. On the various rights of 'outsiders' in Rome, see below, p. 78.

8. A clear account of Athenian citizenship is given by M.M.Austin and P.Vidal-Naquet, *Economic and Social History of Ancient Greece* (London, 1977), 94-103.

of the Republic.[9]

The classification had an individual and collective importance. The ceremony of the census required that each individual citizen declare the precise details of his wealth to the censors in the presence of his fellows. That declaration defined his public status, and was, no doubt, quoted as such on official documents. A preserved papyrus document from a slightly later period provides a clear example: 'L Valerius Crispus, son of Lucius, of the Pollian tribe, *whose census rating is 375,000 sesterces*, declares...'[10]

In its collective aspect the sevenfold division formed the basis of a political structure in which the rich were granted privileged political rights, in particular (by a mechanism we shall discuss below, pp. 50-51) greater voting power than the poor. In the early Republic this had been to some extent balanced by greater obligations on the part of the rich for military service and by a heavier burden of taxation. But after the effective abolition of the land tax in Italy in 167 BC and the development of a 'professional' army, a high census rating carried with it only privileges.[11]

This census classification, which incorporated all male citizens and ranked them, was a central element in Roman political and social life. The amount of scribal effort involved in keeping such records of each citizen and updating them was immense—an administrative labour with few parallels in the ancient world. Yet even more extraordinary to us is the explicit and open economic base this classification gave to the structure of the citizen body. Today we regard the details of a person's earnings and wealth as private information. Tax assessments are marked 'Private and Confidential' and custom dictates that we do not ask even our friends what they earn. We should then be struck by the alien nature of a society in which those details were publicly paraded and directly and formally linked to political rights.[12]

9. Nicolet, *World of the Citizen*, 49-88 lays great stress on the importance of the census; but note the critique of his views in the review by E.Gabba, *JRS* 67 (1977), 192-194. See also T.P.Wiseman, 'The Census in the First Century BC', *JRS* 59 (1969), 59-75, an article whose conclusions spread far beyond the disruption of the census in the last century of the Republic.

10. This document is a formal registration of a birth. For the Latin text, see *Michigan Papyri*, 3 (1936), 154.

11. For the land tax (*tributum*), see Jolowicz and Nicholas, *Roman Law*, 52 and A.H.M.Jones, 'Taxation in Antiquity', in *The Roman Economy* (Oxford, 1974), 161. Livy, *History of Rome*, 1, 42-43 clearly demonstrates the relation of the different *classes* to different military obligations.

12. For the administrative details of the census, see Nicolet, *World of the Citizen*, 60-73. A sculptural representation of the holding of a census (the so-called 'Altar of Domitius Ahenobarbus') is discussed and illustrated by M.Torelli, *Typology and Structure of Roman*

Above the five main census categories came the very top ranks of
Roman society—in top place, the senators; in second, the 'knights'
(*equites*, equestrians). It was these men who controlled the political, legal,
military and economic processes of Rome. How were they defined?
How was entry into their number secured?

In popular parlance any man with a census qualification of over
400,000 sesterces (ten times the qualification for the highest of the five
main grades) was known as an equestrian. These men formed the elite
in the broad sense—and included within their number other smaller,
more prestigious or powerful sets.

The most important of these were the senators—men who began
adult life as equestrians and by securing a position in the senate formed
the political elite of the city. These were the occupants of public office,
the commanders of Rome's armies, the governors of its provinces. We
shall discuss below (pp. 58-61) the role and power of the senate as an
institution. For the moment let us concentrate on its personnel. Up
to the reforms of Sulla (81), senators numbered about 300 men. They
were enrolled, strictly speaking, at the discretion of the censors; but
effectively, at least by the second century BC, they comprised all men
who had held magistracies in the city. Sulla increased the number, by
admitting to the senate about 300 men of equestrian rank. And he
ensured that this number was maintained by enacting that all those
who had held the quaestorship (a junior office and a necessary qualification for further posts) should automatically enter the senate; while
at the same time he raised the number of quaestors elected annually
from ten or so to twenty. The size of the senate was effectively doubled. Yet the senators, of course, remained, even at 600, a tiny proportion of the total population—a tiny proportion with overwhelming
influence and power.[13]

A second set within the elite—of lower formal rank than the
senators—were the *equites* in the strictest sense of the term: not just

Historical Reliefs (Ann Arbor, 1982), 5-16 (or see the photograph in Crawford, *Roman
Republic*, pl.3).
13. On Sulla's reform, see Gabba, *Republican Rome*, 142-150 ('The Equestrian Class and
Sulla's Senate'). We have inclined towards the traditional assumption that right up to
the reforms of Sulla the number of quaestors remained at only 10 (see W.V.Harris, 'The
Development of the Quaestorship, 267-81 BC', *CQ* 26 (1976), 92-106); though E.Badian
is correct to point out ('The Silence of Norbanus: a Note on Provincial Quaestors under
the Republic', *AJPh* 104 (1983), 156-171, esp.168) that this figure is not directly supported
by any ancient evidence. For discussion of the personnel of the Republican senate, see
Gelzer, *Roman Nobility*, 18-27. Note that before the rules were modified in 129, senators
retained their position as equestrians in addition to their senatorial status.

anyone with a qualification of over 400,000 sesterces, but out of those, a select group of 1800 men enrolled into eighteen equestrian 'centuries' at the pinnacle of the census system, above the five main property divisions. Originally these centuries had formed a prestigious cavalry division in the military organisation of the city—the 'century' being in origin the basic unit of the Roman army; but by the late Republic these equestrian centuries no longer had a military function and the evidence for their role is unclear. Some scholars have considered that they had special privileges (for example, as judges in the law courts) separately from the equestrian order in its broader sense. Alternatively it has been argued that these eighteen centuries, while enjoying some voting privileges (see p. 51), had an essentially symbolic or ceremonial role, as representatives of the equestrian order as a whole. We cannot be sure. In any case, the technical distinctions of status within the elite are less important than the fact that it was the equites who with the senators constituted the elite.[14]

Ancient authors and modern historians treat the senate (and to a lesser extent the equestrian order) as if it was, for all practical purposes, an hereditary body. They give the impression that it was exceedingly hard to become a magistrate (and so also a senator) if you did not have a senatorial father, grandfather—and probably a whole string of senatorial ancestors. The senate, in short, appears as exclusive and closed. But image is not always reality. Was it in fact like that?[15]

From the point of view of an individual seeking entry to the senate, it was to some extent a closed order. A 'new man', without senatorial ancestry, would find his path to magistracies both more difficult and slower than a man from a famous aristocratic family. Such an aspirant might understandably have complained at the senate's exclusivity.[16]

---

14. See Brunt, 'Equites', who minimizes the distinction between the eighteen centuries and the equestrian order as a whole. Note also T.P.Wiseman, 'The Definition of 'Eques Romanus' in the Late Republic and Early Empire', *Historia* 19 (1970), 67-83; this article provides the most accessible English discussion of the views of Nicolet, who has argued strongly for important privileges being restricted to the eighteen centuries. More generally, see Gelzer, *Roman Nobility*, 4-18.

15. The image of an exclusive nobility is put forward by Sallust, *Jugurthine War* 63, 6-7; H.H.Scullard, *Roman Politics, 220-150 BC* (Oxford, 1973), 10-12; Syme, *Roman Revolution*, 10-12. See also Hopkins, *Death and Renewal*, 36-40, for a summary of the traditional view and further references.

16. See *A Short Guide to Electioneering* (the *Commentariolum Petitionis*), attributed to Quintus Cicero, for the difficulties encountered by a 'new man' in trying to reach the consulship (especially chaps. 1-14). For a recent review of the controversy over the authenticity of this document, see J.S.Richardson, 'The "Commentariolum Petitionis"', *Historia* 20 (1971), 436-442.

But let us adopt a broader perspective and consider not the problem of any individual, but the general pattern of access to the senate. Here the picture is strikingly different. Analysis of the background of senators in the last two centuries of the Republic suggests that in the lower ranks—that is those senators who did not reach the praetorship—at least a third had a father who had not himself reached the senate; and that even among the most successful senators—those who had reached the praetorship or consulship—one fifth or more were the sons of non-senators. However difficult entry into the senate might appear to individuals, men without recent senatorial ancestry (or no senatorial ancestry at all) did reach the senate in large numbers.[17]

Several factors lay behind this permeability of the senate. The first was demographic. Half the children born were female and mortality (especially among infants) was high at Rome. By using comparative material on death and fertility rates from other better documented societies, we can estimate that between a quarter and a half of senatorial families would have had no son surviving to the age when he might seek the quaestorship. And not all surviving sons would have had either the inclination or the ability to enter a political career. The senatorial order had to recruit members from outside in order to replace itself—and more so in the generation after Sulla, when the size of the senate itself was increased. There was also a plentiful pool of men in the equestrian order ready to fill the gaps: sons, perhaps, of ancient senatorial families which had not reached the senate for generations; the elite of the Italian towns—after their full enfranchisement—keen to make a political career in the capital; men who had benefited from the wealth flowing into Italy, which gave them the resources to enter politics.[18]

There must, in short, have been constant slippage between the senatorial and equestrian orders. Sons of senators failed to reach magistracies—and so remained *equites*. Sons of equestrians reached the senate. While at the bottom of the equestrian order, around the lower limit of 400,000 sesterces, the position must have been similar. Some men would have fallen below the required limit; others, gaining wealth, would have entered the equestrian order for the first time. If at any one moment the boundaries between the orders appeared precisely defined, in a wider context—considered over time—those boundaries were constantly being crossed. And this slippage was especially frequent

17. For the relative 'open-ness' of the Roman elite, see Brunt, '*Nobilitas* and *Novitas*'; Hopkins, *Death and Renewal*, 31-119; Wiseman, *New Men*.
18. For a discussion of mortality rates in the Roman world, see Hopkins, *Death and Renewal*, 69-98.

in the late Republic, a period of rapid imperial expansion, great profits in war and frequent confiscations and death.

The limits of legal status

Some further aspects of status divisions—elided or omitted in our treatment so far—deserve mention. We shall shortly be considering the political institutions of Rome and shall see within them more features of Rome's sharply stratified society. But first let us add some important nuances to the complex system we have already in part discussed.

In the first place, Roman social life was far more multi-faceted than its legal status divisions suggest. These divisions were of the greatest importance, but they did not determine every single form of ranking, nor every form of social interaction. This is particularly clear in the case of senators and *equites*. Modern scholars have tended to treat them as entirely separate groups. They have laid much stress on their undeniably different political roles and the occasional conflicts between them over the control of the jury courts at Rome—and they have even suggested, quite wrongly, that the knights formed a separate commercial class in opposition to a landholding political elite, the senators. We have already referred to the permeability between these two orders. In fact, the economic activities of senators and *equites* were fundamentally similar. *Equites* as well as senators were substantial landowners, as is clearly indicated by the fact that any equestrian who wished to undertake the profitable public contracts which were available had to give surety in land. And underlying this similarity between the two groups there were social and kinship ties between them. The sons of senators who had not attained political office were automatically equestrians; many senators had equestrian fathers and brothers. In these (and many other) cases, different legal rank would not have entailed separation in every context and would not have affected a vast range of common activities: from dinner parties to military service; from involvement in agriculture to the enjoyment of literary culture.[19]

19. Hopkins, *Conquerors and Slaves* 45-47 recognizes the areas of conflict between senators and *equites*, but in general stresses the homogeneity between the two orders. Badian, *Publicans and Sinners*, 82-118 places more emphasis on the clashes between the two. For social contacts between senators and *equites*, the best known example is the friendship between Cicero and Atticus (an equestrian). For a different kind of homogeneity between the two orders, note the claims of J.D'Arms (*Commerce and Social Standing in Ancient Rome* (Cambridge, Mass. and London, 1981), esp. 1-71) that senators, like equestrians, were engaged in commercial enterprises (though contrast the powerful arguments of M.I.Finley, *The Ancient Economy* (London, 1973), 35-61).

In the second place, each legal status category did not necessarily comprise a homogeneous group of men with a common sense of identity. At the top of the hierarchy of status even the small number of senators were divided by power, wealth and prestige. We tend to think of these men as a single category—and, to be sure, their common experience of office holding did set them apart from their fellow citizens. Yet how much would the lower ranks of the senate have felt they shared with their colleagues at the top? At the bottom there were those who had held only junior magistracies in the city. They were known colloquially as *pedarii* (men who vote with their feet) because they were so rarely called upon to speak in the senate and their influence was tiny. At the top were men who had been consuls, had led major military campaigns and governed important provinces. These frequently spoke out and were listened to. The gulf between these two extremes was enormous. A similar gulf must have been evident in other sections of the community. Ex-slaves, for example, formed a single category insofar as they were all subject to certain political disabilities (p. 41); but beyond that they were many and various in their degree of wealth, occupation and social milieu. Few Romans enjoyed the material comfort and social esteem of Cicero's slave, then freedman secretary, Tiro.[20]

Lastly, the significance of individual status divisions might change in the course of time—as was clearly the case with that between patricians and plebeians. In the early Republic these were categories of crucial importance: a small exclusive group of patrician families monopolized all political power and office holding; the remainder of the citizens—plebeians—were by law deprived of these privileges. But gradually this rigid separation was broken down as plebeians won the right to all major offices. By the late Republic the distinction between the two categories was merely vestigial. A small group of patrician families survived—maybe no more than 30 in the 50s BC; but they were not necessarily wealthy nor influential and their particular privileges barely extended beyond the monopoly of one or two priesthoods. Indeed the rich and powerful plebeians of the first century BC (Cicero, Crassus or Pompey, for example) would have laughed at any notion that the plebeians as a group were still second-class citizens in the last centuries

20. For low-ranking senators, see J.R.Hawthorn, 'The Senate after Sulla', *G&R* 9 (1962), 53-60; L.R.Taylor and R.T.Scott, 'Seating Space in the Roman Senate and the *Senatores Pedarii*', *TAPhA* 100 (1969), 529-582. Treggiari, *Freedmen*, 87-161 illustrates the widely different occupations and prestige of different freedmen. We should remember that to a poor man of free birth the life of a rich ex-slave might seem enviable; see, for example, the wealth of the freedman Isidorus, discussed by P.A.Brunt, 'Two Great Roman Landowners', *Latomus* 34 (1975), 619-635.

of the Republic as they had been earlier.[21]

A new form of aristocratic distinction, in fact, took the place of the old rigid division between patricians and plebeians. Alongside senatorial and equestrian status—ranks achieved by individuals through election to office or possession of wealth—there existed in the late Republic a group of men regarded by the ancient sources almost as an hereditary aristocracy. These were the *nobiles* (nobles). The sources make it clear that this group was perceived as the traditional centre of the Roman political elite—men who had a rightful claim on the highest offices of state. Yet they do not make it at all clear how 'nobility' was attained or what qualifications the *nobiles* possessed that others lacked. Certainly it seems that all men whose ancestors included (however far back) a consul were considered 'noble'. So were all patricians and perhaps descendants of other high magistrates—though the edges of the category here are hard to define, and no doubt always were. What matters about this status of nobility is the two-fold shift from the earlier patrician status. First 'nobility' could be acquired by families outside the traditional governing class—Cicero, for example, ennobled his family in perpetuity by winning the consulship. Secondly, 'nobility' carried with it no legal privileges; it was a status, not a legal rank.[22]

Changes in formal status did not always, of course, keep neatly in step with changes in Roman society. A clear time lag may be observed in the extension of Roman citizenship to the rest of Italy. By the time of the Gracchi, Romans and Italians effectively functioned, in military, political and economic terms, as a single society. Yet, the grant of full citizenship to the Italians was delayed for over forty years; and, as we shall see (pp. 80 82) was only conceded after the allies had gone to war against Rome. In practical terms Rome's generosity with her citizenship simply did not keep pace.

Assemblies

The political institutions of Rome often reflected in their structure the formal stratification of Roman society. Nowhere was this more obvious than in the popular assemblies of the city. How did they work? How was the dominance of the elite assured?

21. The early clashes between patricians and plebeians are summarized in Jolowicz and Nicholas, *Roman Law*, 9-17. Cicero, *On his House* 14, 38 runs through the remaining rights and duties of the patricians in the late Republic, though exaggerates (for the sake of his case) their importance.
22. See Brunt, '*Nobilitas* and *Novitas*', who rejects the view put forward by Gelzer (*Roman Nobility*, 27-40) that 'nobility' was confined to the descendants of consuls.

Roman citizens in assembly elected magistrates and gave their approval (or otherwise) to laws presented before them by the magistrates; but they did this in a way quite unfamiliar to us, which seems strange even when compared with other societies in the ancient world. The Athenians in the fifth century, for example, had just one institution called an 'assembly'. Every (male) citizen belonged and each had a vote; and decisions were reached by a simple majority of those votes.[23] By comparison the Roman system was complex. They had four different assemblies, each with a different function - not just one organ of the whole people; and instead of a process whereby a simple majority of votes determined the will of the assembly, there was an intricate system of group voting. All Roman citizens in assembly were divided into groups: the members of each group voted (in secret ballot by the late second century) to produce, by simple majority, the single group vote—that is to say, 500 votes in favour and 501 votes against produced a single group vote of 'No'. The final decision of the whole assembly was determined by the majority of these group votes. As we shall see, it was this two-stage process of group voting in every assembly that allowed the elite to retain a voting power quite disproportionate to their small numbers.[24]

Let us consider the system in action in just one of the Roman assemblies—the 'centuriate assembly' (*comitia centuriata*). This was divided into voting groups called 'centuries'—traditional military divisions—from which it took its name. Its principal function in the late Republic was to elect the most important magistrates of the state.

The centuriate assembly was organized in accordance with the hierarchy of census divisions. It consisted of 193 voting centuries into which men were enrolled on the basis of their property qualification; and these centuries were apportioned between the census 'classes' in such a way that there were many more centuries for the rich than for the poor. All those, for example, who fell below the lowest census 'class' were enrolled into one voting century, while those in the first 'class' (from the mid-third century on) were divided between 70.

This division gave weighted voting influence to the elite, both

23. For an introductory account of the Athenian system of voting in the assembly, see Staveley, *Voting*, 78-93. A more general characterization of Athenian voting and popular participation is given by Finley, *Politics*, 70-84. He also stresses, in a rather extreme contrast, the very limited powers of the Roman assemblies, by comparison with the Athenian.
24. The principle of the group vote and the different types of assembly are clearly discussed by Staveley, *Voting*, 121-142 and Jolowicz and Nicholas, *Roman Law*, 17-30. A convenient table, summarizing the differences between the different assemblies, is provided by Crawford, *Roman Republic*, 196 and Nicolet, *World of the Citizen*, 228.

individually and collectively. The rich were far fewer in number than the poor, yet they were assigned to many more voting units. As a result the number of voters in those units would have been comparatively small—a few hundred in the centuries of the first 'class', compared with many thousands in the bottom century. The arithmetic is obvious: the proportionate influence of a single voter in the first 'class' was many times greater than that of the individual voter in the lower 'classes'.

Collectively too the elite could dominate. In the late Republic there were 18 centuries of equestrians and 70 of the first 'class'. These centuries voted first, and on their own (as 88 out of 193) they almost constituted a majority of the whole assembly. It only needed 9 of the remaining 105 centuries to vote with them, for the wealthy to have their way.[25]

This collective influence of the elite has, however, sometimes been overestimated by modern scholars. Some recent writing can leave the reader wondering why the assembly bothered to meet at all, seeing that the view of the elite was so bound to prevail. We do not wish to underplay the predominant influence of the wealthy in, particularly, the centuriate assembly; but we must stress that this modern approach fails to draw out an important point: that the elite (collectively) could dominate the assembly only if they all voted the same way. For once those top 88 centuries were split, half voting one way and half the other, their collective influence, thus cancelled out, was no greater than that of the poorer citizens. The elite had, in short, a vested interest in unity—which was, of course, not preserved in the political struggles of the late Republic.[26]

The other major assembly of Rome in the late Republic—the 'tribal assembly', organised by geographical districts ('tribes') of Roman citizens—was also liable to the domination of the rich. This was not formally determined, as with the hierarchical census structure of the centuriate assembly; but the practice of Roman politics ensured that the elite retained a preponderance of voting power. The city of Rome itself, for example, where most of the poor had their only home, constituted only 4 out of the 35 tribes. The remaining 31 tribal voting units were formed from the more thinly populated country districts surrounding Rome, where the rich had their landed estates; and probably

25. This assembly is fully discussed by Nicolet, *World of the Citizen*, 219-224, 246-267 and by Taylor, *Roman Voting Assemblies*, 84-106. A large number of articles has been published on a minor reform of the assembly in the third century BC and the interpretation (bearing on that reform) of a disputed passage of Cicero's *On the Republic*. Little useful has come out of this. For the terms of the debate, see E.S.Staveley, 'The Reform of the Comitia Centuriata', *AJPh* 74 (1953), 1-33.
26. For an extreme statement of the orthodox position, see Finley, *Politics*, 91.

only members of the Roman elite had the leisure to travel to Rome to vote and they might even pay to bring in their retainers specially to vote on a particular issue.[27]

But once again we should not exaggerate the influence of the elite, important as it was. Assemblies remained technically, and in Roman perceptions, the organs of the *people*. And it was always possible that poor men from the outlying districts might spontaneously flock to Rome to vote for some proposal which they saw as beneficial—and (given the structure of the tribal assembly) they might carry the day even if the elite was united. This certainly happened, for example, when Tiberius Gracchus introduced his legislation in 133 BC. The dominance of the rich was thus likely, but it was not a foregone conclusion. The poor could not be ignored.[28]

Magistrates

Roman magistrates were political officials elected annually by the popular assemblies. They had different titles according to their different functions and seniority. They held each office for a year, with only very limited possibilities for re-election to the same post. Their power in each magistracy was normally shared with a number of equal colleagues: there was not just one *quaestor*, but a college of *quaestors*.[29]

These facts are important and well known. But on their own they bring us little nearer to understanding how the whole system of office-holding worked; what it meant to undertake a political career; what kind of functions magistrates might fulfil. Let us now consider these issues.

By the mid-second century BC, the magistrates of the Roman people were strictly ordered by seniority. Any man embarking on a political career had to start at the bottom of the series of offices and work his

27. See Nicolet, *World of the Citizen*, 227-234, 246-258. The different power of the urban and rural tribes was clearly recognized by the Romans. Witness the contoversy over which tribes should receive the registration of newly enfranchised freedmen and other new citizens; see L.R.Taylor, *The Voting Districts of the Roman Republic* (Papers and Monographs, American Academy in Rome, 20, Rome, 1960), 101-149; Treggiari, *Freedmen*, 37-52.
28. The presence of poor country voters in Rome when Tiberius Gracchus was introducing his legislation is attested by Appian, *Civil Wars* 1, 10, 41. For a detailed discussion of the origins of the voters, see D.B.Nagle, 'The Failure of the Roman Political Process in 133 BC', *Athenaeum* 48 (1970), 372-394; 49 (1971), 111-128.
29. The principles of Roman magisterial office are clearly laid out by Greenidge, *Roman Public Life*, 152-191 and Loewenstein, *Governance of Rome*, 41-57. A concise survey of the functions of different magistracies is provided by Jolowicz and Nicholas, *Roman Law*, 45-57. For a complete list of known magistrates, year by year, throughout the Republic, see T.R.S.Broughton, *The Magistrates of the Roman Republic*, 2 vols. (New York, 1951 and 1952).

way up—so long as he continued to be elected—in the prescribed order through progressively more senior magistracies. After a required period of military service, the first compulsory office in this series was the quaestorship. From the time of Sulla on, there were twenty such posts open to men who had reached the age of 30. Then in normal sequence—though not strictly compulsory—came the tribunate and/or aedileship. Tribunes, even in the late Republic were always of plebeian status, for the historical reason that their office had been founded in the fifth century to protect the interests of plebeians against patricians; they were ten in number and normally men in their 30s. Aediles, on the other hand, formed a college of four, with a minimum age of 36. Above these offices came the praetorship—eight elected posts open to men of 39 and over; and finally the consulship. Ex-praetors, on reaching the age of 42, might seek election to become one of the two consuls, the chief annual magistrates of the state.[30]

From this rather dry list of qualifications we can draw out two important principles underlying the late Republican system of office-holding.

In first place, it was stratified by age to a degree far greater than in our own society. To be sure, we expect prime ministers and presidents to be at least middle-aged—but we are also used to elections at which elder statesmen fight for the same positions as men and women in their twenties and thirties. That forms a strong contrast with Roman practice—in which a political career consisted, to a great extent, in *constant competition with men of one's own age.* Consider the pattern of life of an aspiring Roman politician of the first century BC. From boyhood he enjoyed close, no doubt rivalrous, links with his direct contemporaries among the elite—at school, at leisure, on military service. When he reached thirty he embarked on fierce public competition with those contemporaries—as they all for the first time became eligible for election to a major public office, the quaestorship. And so it went on through (perhaps) the tribunate, the aedileship (36), praetorship (39) and consulship (42). The age barriers attached to magistracies gave a defining structure to political life: each age group, equal in years, and notionally equal in prestige, progressed together through a series of elections in which they competed with each other for public favour and political power. This principle of peer group competition in the political sphere lies at the heart of the more general competitive ethos

30. On this career structure (*cursus honorum*), see A.Astin, *The Lex Annalis before Sulla* (Coll.Lat.32, Brussels, 1958). E. Badian, 'Caesar's *Cursus* and the Intervals between Offices', *JRS* 49 (1959), 81-89 (repr. in *Studies*, 140-156) discusses possible exceptions to these strict requirements.

of the Roman elite, to which we have already referred (p. 14).

This age-regulated structure of political life had not always been so closely defined. In the less complex society of the earlier Republic the rules of office-holding—in terms of age and order—were more flexible. It was only gradually, by the force of custom and later law, that the distinctive formal structure of the late Republic emerged.[31]

Even in the late Republic the principle of age-group competition did not always operate in so tidy a way as we have implied. The age qualifications were, after all, *minimum* qualifications. The ideal suggested that one should attain office in the first year of one's eligibility; but, in practice, many men must have been delayed in their careers—by failure in elections, lack of resources to mount a campaign, even illness. For men like Cicero, without senatorial ancestry, it was actually noteworthy if they reached high office immediately they were eligible, 'in their own year'. Premature success too disrupted the system. Pompey, for example, during his twenties, had begun to undertake a series of 'emergency commands' overseas, culminating in a major victory in Spain. He then proved unwilling to return to Rome and start, with his erstwhile 'peers', at the bottom of the sequence of elected offices. By threat of violence, he secured election to the consulship of 70 BC at the age of 36, without having held any junior magistracy.[32]

In second place we should observe that the further a man progressed up the political hierarchy, the more intense the competition for office became. By the mid-first century BC there were twenty quaestors in any one year; yet, when their time came, not all of these would be able to win a place among the eight praetors—and even fewer would succeed in gaining election to one of the two consulships at the very top of the hierarchy. This pyramidal structure ensured that at each stage some of those who had started on a political career would fail to progress further. The competition was real; some men lost. Of course, not all of those who had held the quaestorship would necessarily feel inclined to seek higher office; and some ambitious men would have died before

---

31. For an indication of the greater flexibility in the period 366-180 BC, see R. Develin, *Patterns in Office Holding, 366-49 BC* (Coll. Lat. 161, Brussels, 1979), 13-30.

32. For the problems of the *cursus honorum* from the point of view of a new man and the likely delays in his career, see Wiseman, *New Men*, 143-169. The spectacular short cut in Pompey's career is vividly evoked by his total ignorance of procedure in the senate, over which (as consul) he was supposed to preside. He is said to have asked the learned Marcus Terentius Varro to write him a brief guide to senatorial practice (Aulus Gellius, *Attic Nights* 14, 7). Note also the remark of Cicero (*Brutus* 47, 175) that a certain C.Billienus would have reached the consulship had Marius not monopolized the office for so many years—illustrating clear Roman perceptions that the super-successful effectively excluded from office their slightly less successful contemporaries.

they reached the age required for the praetorship or consulship. Nevertheless, it is clear that, even when such 'dropouts' are taken into account, the competition for the consulship was more intense than that for the praetorship; and the competition for the praetorship more intense than that for the quaestorship.[33]

Political 'careers'

We have talked so far about a Roman political 'career', as if it were roughly comparable with a modern political (or business or academic) 'career'. In fact the word is inappropriate in the context of Roman politics for many reasons. Let us make some comparisons.

It is a reasonable assumption today that a career brings with it a salary. Yet no Roman politician received pay for undertaking office—and in fact many magistracies involved the holder in considerable expense. Aediles, for example, had the responsibility of organizing the *ludi* (games), celebrations in honour of the gods, which included chariot racing, gladiatorial shows and theatrical performances. Some money was provided by the state to stage these events; but to present the kind of lavish spectacle that was increasingly expected, the magistrates were forced to contribute much from their own pockets. With luck, of course, such cost might be recouped. It was well recognised in the late Republic that Roman officials in the provinces had many opportunities—through outright theft or extortion, manipulation of the tax system and so forth —to grow rich at the expense of the local inhabitants.[34]

We also readily assume that a 'career' is the occupation of a working life—typically practised 5 days a week, 48 weeks a year for 40 years or so. A Roman politician, however, had no such full-time job. He held magistracies for just one year at a time; and between each office there were gaps of several years. Of course, he was not necessarily politically inactive in the intervening periods. Besides meetings of the senate and various informal ways of exercising political influence (such as

33. The 'reality' of defeat is illustrated by the career of Catiline, who was twice defeated at election for the consulship. See the clear (but rather dated) narrative of E.G.Hardy, *The Catilinarian Conspiracy in its Context: a Re-study of the Evidence* (Oxford, 1924), 21-30, 39-48.
34. Note the expenses of the aedilate of M.Scaurus (58 BC) (mentioned by Cicero, *On Duties* 2, 16, 57 and Pliny, *Natural History* 36, 24, 113-115) and the trouble taken by M.Caelius to secure a set of panthers from the East for his games in 50 (Cicero, *Letters to Friends* 8, 9 (Shackleton Bailey 79), 3 and Stockton, *Cicero*, 229-230). The possibilities for extortion are vividly evoked by Cicero's speeches *Against Verres*; likewise Catullus 10 illustrates the *assumption* that money could be made in the provinces. For a clear discussion of the expenses of office and the profits that could be made in the provinces, see I.Shatzman, *Senatorial Wealth and Roman Politics* (Coll. Lat. 142, Brussels, 1975), 53-67 and 159-167.

pleading in the law courts—see pp. 65-66), the extra posts available from the second century BC on in the government and administration of Rome's growing empire tended to erode the gap between offices. In particular the system of *pro*magistracies—whereby after a year in elected office a magistrate went abroad to govern a province *pro* (in place of) a regular praetor or consul—considerably lengthened the time an individual might spend directly occupied in state business. Nevertheless, the normal pattern of office holding right through the Republic remained spasmodic. The careers of such men as Pompey and Caesar, who managed, in the final crises of the Republic, to occupy office almost continuously, were anomalous; in themselves they represented a threat to traditional Republican norms.[35]

But the most important fact about a Roman politician was that he was not a 'specialist'. This again contrasts sharply with our own notions of 'career'. For modern professions (engineering, medicine, law, for example) entail almost by definition the acquisition of special, narrowly defined skills. Roman magistrates, on the other hand, were traditionally all-rounders in the most general sense. Let us consider for a moment their range of duties. What might a Roman magistrate have found himself doing?

Some of their responsibilities we would term administrative or political: supervision of market arrangements; supervision of state archives; responsibility for the city finances and corn supply; summoning of popular assemblies or the senate; the proposal of legislation; the explanation and discussion of proposed legislation with the people in less formal meetings, known as *contiones*; the conduct of elections; the government of provinces. The list could go on and on.[36]

These Roman administrators and politicians were, however, also military men. It would seem hardly conceivable to us that the same individual should one minute be at a desk, say as an economist at the treasury, and the next be commanding the British fleet in a naval battle. But just such a variety of duties was laid upon Roman officials. As magistrates (or in the first century BC, generally as promagistrates) it was assumed that they were competent to take military or naval

35. A clear account of promagistracies and the developments of the late Republic is provided by G.H.Stevenson, *Roman Provincial Administration till the Age of the Antonines* (Oxford, 1939), 55-66. For a detailed history of the system of promagistracies, see W.F.Jashemski, *The Origins and History of the Proconsular and Propraetorian Imperium to 27 BC* (Chicago, 1950). J.Richardson, *Roman Provincial Administration, 227 BC—AD 117* (London, 1976), 27-46 offers an introduction to Roman provincial government intended for school students.
36. For the variety of magistrates' tasks, see Greenidge, *Roman Public Life*, 191-237. On *contiones*, in particular, see Nicolet, *World of the Citizen*, 285-289; Taylor, *Roman Voting Assemblies*, 15-33.

command—maybe against hostile tribes in Asia Minor or Spain; maybe against pirates near Crete. Military responsibilities were intertwined with civilian.[37]

Roman magistrates also played a major role in administering the law. Not only did they enjoy the right of summary punishment over the petty criminal in the street, but they also operated the system of criminal and civil courts. From the mid-second century on, special jury courts (*quaestiones*) were developed at Rome to deal with particular major crimes defined by statute—extortion, treason, electoral bribery, murder and so forth. These courts sat under the presidency of magistrates, usually praetors; but the power of the magistrate did not extend beyond controlling the proceedings in the court and declaring the verdict of the jury.[38]

In the 'civil law' (that is the 'private law' of disputes between individuals over such matters as property, inheritance, contract and defamation) the power of the magistrates was greater. Here the rules of law were partly defined by statute, but partly (as in many societies) they depended on tradition and were not, even in the first century BC, fully codified. The magistrate in charge of the 'civil courts'—in Rome, always one of the praetors—was able, during his year of office, to expound and develop the 'civil law' by his power to 'give an action' (that is 'to allow a case to go before a judge') and also to issue injunctions, to grant possession of property to people, and so on. An example typical of the day-to-day legal duties of a praetor in the first century BC will make this power clearer.

Suppose, for example, Marcus had sold something to Gaius, but had not been paid. Marcus would bring his opponent before the praetor, who heard the complaints and counter-arguments of each side; and it was up to the praetor to decide whether or not he would 'give an action'. In making this decision he might go beyond the scope of legal precedent and effectively adapt the traditional body of law to fit new circumstances. If an 'action' was granted, then, in the presence

---

37. Note that even the most 'unmilitary' Cicero found himself in a province, commanding an army; and he came to desire a triumph for his victory. See Stockton, *Cicero*, 236-239 and M.Wistrand, *Cicero Imperator: Studies in Cicero's Correspondence, 51-47 BC* (Studia Graeca et Latina Gothoburgensia 41, Göteborg, 1979), 1-60.
38. For a simple account of the *quaestiones*, see Jolowicz and Nicholas, *Roman Law*, 318-320. A detailed account of the procedure of these courts is given by A.H.J.Greenidge, *The Legal Procedure of Cicero's Time* (Oxford, 1901, repr. New York, 1971), 415-525, and of the history of the extortion court in particular by J.P.V.D.Balsdon, 'The History of the Extortion Court at Rome, 123-70 BC', *PBSR* 14 (1938), 98-114 (repr. in Seager, *Crisis*, 132-148). See also E.S.Gruen, *Roman Politics and the Roman Criminal Courts, 149-78 BC* (Cambridge, Mass., 1968), although Gruen overstresses the 'factional' element in Roman politics (see below, pp. 67-68).

of the praetor, the exact issue to be settled and the precise terms of reference for the trial were decided; and finally a private citizen was appointed as judge (*iudex*), or, for other sorts of civil action it might be a group of judges (*recuperatores*) or a large jury (*centumviri*). It was these men who then issued judgment on the case and the praetor played no further part.[39]

The praetor, when making important legal decision, no doubt consulted men who had made themselves learned in the law and who were available to give advice to magistrates or private citizens. Yet the formal power of decision-making was not passed over to legal experts. The magistrates here filled what we would regard as a 'specialist' legal role, without being in the modern sense 'specialists'.[40]

We come finally to consider the senate, the council which, by the final phase of the Republic, comprised all men who had held the office of quaestor—perhaps about 600 in all. We have already discussed in some detail its personnel and the status of *senators* as a group; and we have stressed (pp. 34-35) the important role of the senate as the focus of communication between men and gods. It remains to discuss the council's role more generally within the institutional and political structure of the state.

The senate was the only 'permanent' council of Rome—made up of lifelong members (over the age of 30) and meeting perhaps 40 times a year. As such it represented the only element of institutional continuity in Roman politics. But precisely how? For what exact purpose? It was certainly quite unlike the Civil Service in modern Britain—which represents an element of *administrative* continuity above the swings of party politics. Nor did it function like the Council of 500 in Athens, the *boulê*—whose primary purpose was to prepare and order business for the popular assembly. The senate itself did not undertake the business of drafting proposals, though magistrates were normally expected to consult them before presenting legislation to an assembly. Modern writers have generally agreed, in fact, that the role of the senate was that of a 'consultative body', an 'advisory council' of senior politicians. That is no doubt true—but as a definition it seems hopelessly unspecific and hardly helps to explain the apparent importance of the senate in

39. For further discussion of this legal procedure, especially the role of the praetor, see Crook, *Law and Life*, 73-85 and Nicolet, *World of the Citizen*, 334-341. In greater detail, see A.Watson, *Law Making in the Later Roman Republic* (Oxford, 1974), 31-100.
40. For legal science and the role of legal 'experts' in the late Republic, see F.Schulz, *History of Roman Legal Science* (Oxford, 1946), 38-98. It is usually supposed that it was the advice given to magistrates by men learned in the law that lay behind the sophisticated development of Rome's legal system.

the late Republic.[41]

Contemporary observers certainly saw in the senate the most important organ of the state. Cicero, for example, claimed that the senate
was intended to be 'the saviour, defender and protector of the state'
and that the magistrates were, in a sense, the 'servants' of this 'imposing council', while a century earlier Polybius had claimed that the senate
was in effect the body which controlled the Roman world. They were
agreed that the senate was what mattered.[42]

Yet, if we look at the formal powers of the senate, it is difficult to
understand quite how it occupied a position of such centrality. To be
sure it had a range of (individually) important functions: consultation
with magistrates before they put legislation to the people; the declaration of 'states of emergency' at times of extreme crisis—the so-called
'Senatus Consultum Ultimum'; negotiation with foreign ambassadors;
the right to sanction special expenditure—on, for example, important
military campaigns; and so forth. But still the sum of these parts does
not seem, at least on paper, overwhelmingly impressive—a feeling rein-
forced when we consider the powers it did *not* have. Most notably
throughout the Republic, on a strict constitutional definition, its decrees
lacked the force of law.[43]

The role of the senate remains a problem for modern historians.
In terms of its specifically defined functions, it is almost impossible
to see why Polybius and Cicero talk as they do. Let us therefore post-
pone further discussion of the senate until the next chapter—in which
we shall consider in greater detail not so much the structure but the
practical working of these institutions.

---

41. For an introductory discussion of the senate,its composition and function, see Jolowicz
and Nicholas, *Roman Law*, 30-45. The strictly *advisory* role of the senate is brought out
by Wirszubski, *Libertas*, 21. For the primarily 'probouleutic' functions of the Athenian
boulê, see J.M.Moore, *Aristotle and Xenophon on Democracy and Oligarchy* (2nd ed., London, 1982), 185-186, 276-280.
42. See Cicero, *On Behalf of Sestius* 65, 137 and Polybius, *Histories* 6, 13.
43. For the formal powers of the senate, see Greenidge, *Roman Public Life*, 272-288 and
Loewenstein, *Governance of Rome* 161-168. For the constitutional position and significance
of the 'Senatus Consultum Ultimum', see Finley, *Politics*, 3-6; Lintott, *Violence*, 149-174;
Wirszubski, *Libertas*, 55-61.

Chapter Five

THE WORKING OF POLITICS

The functioning of the institutions of the Roman Republic may seem as alien to us as their structure. Let us start with the working of the body which, as we have just seen, was regarded as the central institution of the Roman state—the senate. The senate was in a very different position from the other elements of the Roman state. If a consul told an army to do something, it usually obeyed; if the people passed a law, its prescriptions were usually observed. The senate, by contrast, had very few formal powers; even on uncontroversial matters, and even before the age of revolution, strictly speaking it only *advised* magistrates on what they should do and *advised* on legislation. Advisory powers no doubt carried weight in periods of consensus; but they were not always enough in periods of political conflict, such as that at the end of the Republic.[1]

Let us take a concrete example of the inadequacy of the traditional advisory approach. Major problems of the late Republic stemmed from the powers granted to individual generals; for there was a clash between the view, on the one hand, that they should act under instruction from the senate and the necessity, on the other, that they should be granted considerable freedom of action and personal responsibility in order to cope with Rome's enemies. In the last resort a powerful general could ignore the senate—as Julius Caesar did in Gaul in the 50s. When the senate declined to authorise the treasury to pay for additional legions, he simply paid for them himself. Slightly earlier, Pompey had not quite got away with similar conduct. Between 66 and 63 he had annexed much of the east to the Roman empire without consulting the senate; but this body, spurred on by his political enemies, insisted on discussing his arrangements on his return. His resentment over this insistence played a part in encouraging him to ally with Caesar in 60 (pp. 1,17).[2]

---

1. This advisory function is implicit in the term *senatus consultum*; although normally translated 'decree of the senate', it means rather 'expression of opinion of the senate'.
2. For a lucid account of the position of Caesar in Gaul, see M.Gelzer, *Caesar* (Oxford,

Yet even in the last century of the Republic—as we have seen in the writings of Polybius and Cicero—the traditional authority of the senate was to some extent maintained. This derived from two factors, neither of which involved the exercise of specific powers.

In the first place there remained a sense that for a long time the upper orders of the Roman state had been in essential agreement on all important matters and that the senate was the place where the agreement had been expressed. This fact alone gave the senate tremendous symbolic and practical importance; in the late Republic it was the only area in which consensus might still *conceivably* be achieved.

Secondly the senate remained a force for integration in Roman society. Membership of the senate was something to which, in theory, any freeborn Roman might aspire. And those who were members had gained their membership because the people *as a whole* had at an earlier stage voted them into office. Once achieved, the status of senator was permanent—as opposed to the very temporary accolade represented by winning a magistracy.[3]

This integrating role is of crucial importance in understanding the position of the senate; and it may be seen in the context of two more general considerations of political practice. Highly stratified societies, such as Rome, if they are to function at all, must forge links between their various layers; these cannot remain in isolation, nor in constant opposition. Likewise, highly competitive elites, as the Roman political elite certainly was, must be able to suspend competition and emphasise the existence of stable long-term cohesion. Both of these political needs were in part met by the Roman Republican senate.

We turn now to a broader discussion of the workings of late Republican politics. The subject is vast; so we have chosen to concentrate on four principal questions. The first two relate closely to issues broached in our treatment of the senate: that is, what factors served to link the different layers of Roman society? and what areas of political activity allowed or encouraged continuity and cohesion? The second pair are two of the most important and difficult problems of Roman Republican political history: that is, what kind of motivation lay behind

---

1968), 102-194, esp. 123-124; Brunt, *Italian Manpower*, 466-468.

3. Senators could in theory be and sometimes were ejected for moral turpitude by the censors, and they could also lose their position as a result of condemnation for certain offences; see Jolowicz and Nicholas, *Roman Law*, 52-53 and Hopkins, *Death and Renewal*, 74-75. Neither fate was common—the censorship of 70 was quite exceptional in ejecting 64 senators, whose attempts to regain their position by winning elective office once more contributed much to the intensity of political competition in the 60s.

the actions of Roman politicians, and why did the relatively stable politics of the early second century BC collapse in the first century into repeated civil war? In short, what went wrong?

Cohesion

One obvious way in which links were formed between members of the Roman elite and men of lesser status was in the relationship of patronage. This institution had its origins in the earliest period of Rome's history. The client, in those early days, was a man of inferior status who depended on his patron for personal and economic protection; in return he was expected to serve the interests of his patron, perhaps to labour for him and to act in a way that was overtly deferential. This was a primitive and, sometimes no doubt, oppressive form of quasi-legal personal subservience.

The patron on his side, however, did have clear obligations. In particular he was expected to defend his clients at law. This was already defined as a legal obligation on him in the so-called 'Twelve Tables' of the mid-fifth century BC, the first, partial, codification of Roman law; and from the second century onwards, as the development of legislation led to the definition of a more complex variety of offences, that obligation became even more important. Indeed, by the time of Cicero, one meaning of the word 'patronus' was simply 'advocate'.[4]

But how like in general to its original form was the institution of patronage in the late Republic? How pervasive an institution was it?

The sharp edge of oppression was certainly blunted by the first century BC, although strict ties of formal economic dependence continued in the relationship between ex-slaves and their former masters. But though the bonds of obligation between patron and client were looser, they were still of crucial importance in many areas of social life. The powerful politician in the final centuries of the Republic needed the services—and especially the votes—of his clients more than ever before; he might even need their bodies to serve in his army. In return—in addition to the legal protection expected of the patron—the client who himself aspired to move up the ladder of a political career could call on the help of his patron at the start of that competitive struggle.

---

4. For an account of the traditional relationship between patron and client, see A.Watson, *Rome of the Twelve Tables* (Princeton, 1975), 98-104. The position in the late Republic is clearly discussed by Crook, *Law and Life*, 93-94. As Finley rightly remarks (*Politics* 41), the notion of *fides* (mutual obligation) between client and patron has often been overstressed, even romanticized. See, for example, Taylor, *Party Politics*, 41-42.

Patronage, as a link between men of higher and lower status, was embedded in the patterns of political life.[5]

Of course, the sheer size of the Roman state from at least the fourth century BC meant that there can have been no direct relationship of clientship between the (few) members of the Roman elite and the hundreds of thousands of ordinary citizens in Rome and Italy. In laying bare the structure of the institution, our account has tended to oversimplify. We must suppose instead a more complex model, in which an individual might well be both the client of one or two more powerful men and also himself the patron of many others more lowly. The relationship of patron and client produced chains of connections through Roman society, in the city itself and, in later periods, in Italy and the provinces. It was not just a simple link between the high and the low—but it operated between the strata of Roman society to link, say, the rank and file senator with the most powerful consul or the struggling peasant to the nearby farmer.[6]

Links between the Roman elite and the Roman people were also forged in fields of joint activity. The foremost of these was undoubtedly war. We tend to think of Roman armies as comprised essentially of two separate elements—powerful generals and their immediate entourage on the one hand, and the rank and file soldiery on the other. They come together in our minds (as in traditional history books) only at the beginning of campaigns, when the general recruited his army, and at the end, when he fulfilled his obligations to his troops by distributing booty and, in some cases, land. We forget that war must be, in part, a cooperative activity and that between the highest and the lowest ranks a range of intermediate grades (our 'junior officers' or 'NCOs') provided a bridge. If the rigid separation existing in our minds had existed in Roman armies, Roman victories would have been much less frequent![7]

In fact, ambitious young men of the Roman elite were obliged to undertake military service. In the time of Polybius, a man had to serve for ten campaigns as a junior officer before he was allowed to seek

5. On freedmen, see Crook, *Law and Life*, 51-55 and Treggiari, *Freedmen*, 68-81. Note the case of L.Domitius Ahenobarbus, who manned seven ships against Caesar in 49 with his slaves, freedmen and *coloni* (tenants) (Caesar, *Civil War* 1, 34). For the electoral role of clients, see Quintus Cicero, *A Short Guide to Electioneering* 17. An example of a political career begun under the patronage of greater men is that of Marius (p. 7), who was helped to his early offices by the Metelli (Plutarch, *Life of Marius* 4, 1).
6. For the Italian dimension to the institution of patronage, see Badian, *Foreign Clientelae*, 141-153; Wiseman, *New Men*, 38-47, 130-42.
7. For the army of the late Republic see R.E.Smith, *Service in the Post-Marian Roman Army* (Manchester, 1958); on the importance of centurions and other intermediate grades, L.Keppie, *The Making of the Roman Army: from Republic to Empire* (London, 1984), 176-180.

election to the lowest offices in the hierarchy of magistracies at Rome. This was a period during which he would necessarily be involved in prolonged contact with members of the lower orders. And even if the *formal* obligation to serve for ten campaigns had fallen into abeyance by the time of Cicero, considerable military service was still expected of young aristocrats. Cicero himself served as a junior officer during the Social War (pp. 80-82). Military service remained a shared activity of elite and people.[8]

Similarly elite and people acted together in exploiting the fruits of their conquest. They joined, for example, in planting settlements on land in Italy taken from their conquered enemies, and, as Roman control spread to embrace the entire Mediterranean, they participated together in milking the provinces. No doubt the senatorial and equestrian orders gained most out of this exploitation; but it would not have been possible without the work and cooperation of the lower orders. To take an extreme example, the system of tax collection simply could not have functioned if the governor and his staff had not occasionally talked to the low-ranking employees (often ex-slaves) of the companies of tax collectors.[9]

The Roman electoral system also united the elite and the people. We have already argued (above, pp. 51-52) that the disproportionate influence of the highest orders in Roman elections has often been exaggerated by modern scholars. Now let us take this further: ambitious members of the Roman elite *depended* on the Roman people for what mattered most in their careers—election to a series of magistracies. That dependence influenced the character of the relation between the higher and lower orders.

An anecdote concerning Scipio Nasica (consul 138 BC) illustrates what we mean. As candidate for the office of aedile (above, p.53), Nasica was shaking hands with voters in an effort to win support. He noticed that one man's hands were horny—from manual labour in the fields— and asked him, as a joke, if he usually walked on them. The peasant on-lookers heard this and took offence, believing that Nasica was insulting their poverty. The story spread, among the country voters in particular—and Nasica lost the election! Whether or not this story is strictly true, it was no doubt believable. Roman politicians—at least at election time—insulted the Roman commons at their peril.[10]

---

8. Nicolet, *World of the Citizen*, 89-109, documents the continuing importance of military service in the late Republic.

9. For Roman colonization, see E.T.Salmon, *Roman Colonisation under the Republic* (London, 1969). For the companies of tax-collectors, see below, pp. 70 and 75.

10. The anecdote is recorded by Valerius Maximus (early first century AD), *Anecdotes* 7, 5, 2, and discussed by Hopkins, *Death and Renewal*, 107-116. On the reliability of anecdotes

The institution of the tribunate also demonstrates how far the Roman people were seen to have a claim on the Roman elite. This magistracy was not a compulsory stage of the regular series of offices. Yet it was often held in the late Republic by rich, ambitious young aristocrats. The only specific qualification which reflected its origin—as a protection for the plebeians against the power of the patricians in the fifth century BC (above, p. 48)—was that of plebeian status; members of the few remaining patrician families were excluded from holding the office. Yet, however rich and aristocratic some of the holders of this magistracy may have been, the office itself always retained a popular character. Tribunes, for example, had the right to prevent a magistrate punishing a citizen; they could veto the decisions of magistrates and senate; they were required to be perpetually accessible—with doors open day and night—to any citizen who wished to appeal for their aid. These, and other such powers, were of great importance and their use has been the subject of much modern discussion. For the moment let us note just one point: that many young Roman politicians, of noble birth, held a magistracy which put them in a special relationship with the Roman commons. Whatever their personal inclinations, the tribunate—by its powers and obligations as an office—defined their role for a year as one on which the people had a call. This formed a further institutional link between the elite and people.[11]

Expressions of continuity

We now turn to consider areas of continuity in Roman politics and areas where the cohesion of the Roman elite might find expression. The senate, as we have suggested (above, p. 61), was one such area. There were others; but they were areas which, while 'political' in the Roman context, were by and large not those which we today associate with political activity.

The law courts provided one of the contexts in which a man's political alignment might be observed with some degree of continuity. The

---

in general, see R.P.Saller, 'Anecdotes as Historical Evidence for the Principate', *Greece and Rome* 27 (1980), 69-83 Although focussed on the early empire, many points raised in this article apply equally to the late Republic.
11. For the role of the tribune as 'protecter' of individual citizens, Wirszubski, *Libertas*, 24-27 and, in greater detail, A.W.Lintott, 'Provocatio: from the Struggle of the Orders to the Principate', in *ANRW* 1, 2 (1972), 226-267, esp. 228-231. On the traditional and symbolic links of tribunician power and the plebs, see Z.Yavetz, *Plebs and Princeps* (Oxford, 1968), 54-57.

activity of pleading in the law courts was not the job of 'professional' lawyers; advocacy was one of the skills expected of most members of the Roman elite and it was essentially political. Not only did it provide an important vehicle for political advancement, because the advocate could later count on the political support of those whom he had successfully defended. Not only did some of the cases reaching the law courts arise directly out of a political context—such as that of Cicero's client, Sextus Roscius, accused of murder during the atrocities which marked the dictatorship of Sulla. The law courts quite simply provided a regular and open public platform for an orator, and the major cases heard—even those which were not explicitly political—almost always had political overtones. For the all-round nature of a Roman political career (above, pp. 55-59) meant that every aspect of the life of a politician under trial—from his treatment of provincials to his drinking habits—was politically relevant. Almost every case the advocate handled thus provided the opportunity, however indirect, for the statement of a political position.[12]

An important arena for the expression of cohesion within groups of the Roman elite was the *consilium*—the advisory 'council' of relatives and associates on which members of the Roman elite depended for support and guidance. This institution is crucial to any understanding of the actions of Roman politicians in the late Republic; but because it did not have the formal or permanent constitution of, for example, the assemblies, it is often forgotten.[13]

Any prominent Roman was expected to consult his relatives and associates—as his *consilium*—before making any important decision. The final decision remained his, and he was not bound by any formal majority vote, but his obligation to consult was absolute. Thus the head of a family would consult other members of the family before invoking the powers he had over his children; Tiberius Gracchus consulted his friends and advisers before embarking on his legislative programme in 133; a magistrate in the provinces would take the advice of his entourage before making important decisions; and Brutus called a despairing gathering of his family and friends (including his mother, half sister, wife, Cassius and Cicero) after the murder of Caesar did not immediately bring about the restoration of normal government. This traditional obligation to consult stands in contrast to the

12. See J.M.Kelly, *Roman Litigation* (Oxford, 1968), 31-68. On the role of the courts in the rise of Cicero, see Taylor, *Party Politics*, 98-118.
13. The Republican *consilium* is discussed by J.A.Crook, *Consilium Principis* (Cambridge, 1955), 4-7.

perpetually competitive ethos of the Roman elite, that we have previously stressed. As with the senate (which was in a sense the *consilium* of the two consuls), it provided an institutional framework for cohesion among Roman politicians, a setting for cooperation and alliance.[14]

Motivation

The problem of the motivation of Roman politicians is complicated. All kinds of factors influence people's conduct and we can never be sure why, in any individual case, they act as they do. Yet we can look for general trends. Here we want principally to suggest that one influential strand in recent writing—which seeks to understand Roman politics in terms of a struggle for power between groups based on family loyalty—is almost wholly mistaken.[15]

This popular view is flawed for many reasons. Relatives by blood and marriage did, of course, often act together and sometimes united into groups to achieve common ends. But it is a caricature of Roman politics to hold that men acted as they did *because* they belonged to a particular family group and *because* they simply wished that group to come out on top. Nor is any such view compatible with the evidence we have: relatives did not always support each other. Consider the experience of Tiberius Gracchus. The group of supporters whom he summoned for advice certainly included a relative by marriage, Appius Claudius Pulcher, but another relative, Publius Scipio Aemilianus, was bitterly opposed to what he was trying to do. And in the civil wars at the end of the Republic many members of the same families fought on different sides. There was no straightforward and predictable system of family loyalties.[16]

14. For the powers of a head of a family, see Crook, *Law and Life*, 107-113. The most revealing account of the senate as the *consilium* of the consuls is that given by Cicero in the course of his account of the debates in 91 over the proposal to enfranchise the Italians (pp. 80-82), *On the Orator* 3, 1, 1—2, 8.

15. For analyses of Roman politics in these terms see (for the middle Republic) H.H.Scullard, *Roman Politics, 220-150 BC* (2nd ed., Oxford, 1973), with a discussion of problems of method at xvii-xxiii; and (for the late Republic) Taylor, *Party Politics*. Likewise Syme's *Roman Revolution* largely ignores ideological considerations in its narrative of the fall of the Republic. For a general discussion of the method underlying the approaches of these authors, see L.Stone, 'Prosopography', *Daedalus*, Winter 1971, 46-79. An important critique of an influential German work with a similar approach is offered by P.A.Brunt, 'Review and Discussion of Chr.Meier, *Res Publica Amissa*' (Wiesbaden, 1966), in *JRS* 58 (1968), 229-232. R.Seager has pointed out ('Factio', *JRS* 62 (1972), 53-58) that the Latin word often translated as 'faction' is not used in antiquity to mean 'a political group'.

16. See D.R.Shackleton Bailey, 'The Roman Nobility in the Second Civil War', *CQ* 10 (1960), 253-267, for relatives fighting on opposite sides.

A further point which undermines the view that Roman politics was essentially a power struggle between rival families is found in Roman accounts of politics in all periods, but particularly the age of revolution. For these systematically present political conflict as being about 'real issues', about access by the people to the rewards of conquest and the creating of the political means to achieve this end. It is, of course, possible to argue that these accounts simply provide a political rationalization for family power struggles; but we believe that it is, in fact, difficult to *make sense* of Roman politics without incorporating issues of ideology that transcended family allegiance.[17]

Consider again the attempted reforms of Tiberius Gracchus and the events surrounding his death (pp. 4-6). Principles were surely at stake here. A new situation—a large number of citizens without sufficient (or any) land—appeared to some politicians to demand a new solution: the distribution of state land. Others believed that to meet that demand—especially through the decision of the popular assembly—would mean the end to the system whereby material advantages flowed to the lower orders essentially as an act of goodwill by the elite. They felt, no doubt, that the destruction of the traditional system was a greater ill than the ill which Ti. Gracchus set out to remedy. There is a significant opposition here. We need to understand these opposing ideologies in order to understand not only the violence of the reaction to Gracchus' methods and reforms, but also the conduct of his younger brother and later figures who tried to devise ways in which representatives of the people could get what the people wanted. Family loyalties may have counted for something, but certainly not everything.

Breakdown

So what went wrong with the working of politics in the last years of the Republic? Once again, this is a question of great complexity to which there is no single easy answer. In this section we shall think in terms of political competition and show how the breakdown of stable political life was related first of all to a dramatic explosion in the traditional forms of competition and secondly to the emergence in the late Republic of new forms of competition. This emphasis on *competition*

17. For a critique of simplistic views of political friendship, see P.A.Brunt, '*Amicitia* in the Late Roman Republic', *PCPhS* 11 (1965), 1-20 (repr. in R.Seager, *Crisis*, 199-218). Some important ideological concepts are discussed by Wirszubski, *Libertas*, 1-96; R.Seager, 'Cicero and the Word *Popularis*', CQ 22 (1972), 328-338; Finley, *Politics*, 97-141 (a comparative study of Greece and Rome).

is not meant to undermine what we have already said about the importance of political ideology in the late Republic. A man's support of
a particular political position was integrally bound up with his own
success and glory.

Let us remember at the outset (as we have stressed before, pp. 55-
56) that even the most active and successful members of the elite held
offices of the Roman state for only a small proportion of their adult
lives. A system in which a man might have just one year in which to
make his mark was bound to involve, even in periods of consensus,
a high level of competition. Its very structure would tend to diminish
the scrupulousness of politicians: the *methods* by which glory is achieved
are of secondary importance if the competition is intense.[18]

Yet the late Republic witnessed an escalation in even the high level
of competition embedded within the Roman political structure. There
were two main reasons for this.

First, the value of the prizes to be won grew in absolute terms. Election to office might now lead to a military command in, say, the eastern
Mediterranean, where victory would be likely to bring immense wealth
and immense prestige. The gap between the successful and the non-
successful politician widened; failure became even more devastating,
and winning—no matter how—more important.[19]

Secondly, the reforms of Sulla made the intensity of competition for
high office even greater in the final phase of the Republic. Sulla had
doubled the number of quaestors elected each year from ten to twenty;
while he added only two to the college of praetors (making a total of
eight instead of six) and retained a consulship comprised of just two
men. More men than ever before, entering the quaestorship, would
have had their hopes of a political career raised; more than ever before
would have found the higher echelons of that career impossible to reach.
This kind of career 'blockage' (only partially relieved by the early death
of some of those involved) had obvious consequences.

As the competition became more intense (and as the stakes in that
competition grew), more members of the Roman elite were prepared
to resort to illicit tactics to secure the offices they wanted. The *institutions* of the middle Republic may have remained intact, but they were

18. See J.A.North, 'The Development of Roman Imperialism', *JRS* 71 (1981), 1-9, for
an illustration of this point in the context of the expansion of the Roman empire.
19. Even in 'peaceful' provinces, the acquisition of wealth was often at the expense of
the provincials. The classic case of extortion is provided by Caius Verres, governor of
Sicily, prosecuted by Cicero in 70; see Cicero's series of speeches *Against Verres*. Badian's
Roman Imperialism and *Publicans and Sinners* provide numerous illustrations of other enor-
mities in the late Republican government of the empire.

by-passed as ambitious politicians found that violence was a more effective way of achieving their goals—magistracies or the passage of contentious laws.[20]

By the last decades of the Republic, disruption of political life went beyond this mere by-passing of institutions. For violence, or the threat of violence, had so eroded the system that much of the machinery of government simply did not function for long periods. Political leaders (such as Bibulus, pp. 37-38) were prevented from going to meetings for fear of their lives; the new year sometimes opened with major magistrates still not elected, because of constant (potentially violent) obstruction of elections. The explosion of competition now threatened to extinguish the political system from which it had grown.[21]

New forms of competition also emerged in the late Republic, and the areas to which competition extended grew in number. Newly acquired provincial territory, for example, provided a whole new field of operation—as is made clear in the career of Pompey. By building up a special relationship with many communities in the eastern empire, as a patron on the grandest scale, he used his obvious power outside Rome as a factor in his political manoeuvring in the city. In 52, indeed, he was simultaneously governor of Spain (which he never visited and which his staff ran for him) and consul in Rome.

Likewise the development of specialized organs of government created yet further areas of conflict. We have already mentioned the role of *publicani* as tax collectors in the provinces (p. 64), and we shall have more to say of their fabulous profits (p. 75). Let us bear in mind that these men could find themselves at odds with provincial governors. The technical arrangements for tax collecting on a large scale were complicated and provided many potential areas for quarrel. Indeed in some cases such quarrels resulted (directly or indirectly) in the prosecution of the governor when he returned to Rome. An

---

20. The activities of P.Clodius and T.Annius Milo provide an extreme case of the use of violence in politics, see Stockton, *Cicero*, 194-226. In addition to the articles cited at p. 9, n.16, note A.W.Lintott, 'Cicero and Milo', *JRS* 64 (1974), 62-78. For a somewhat different perspective, see P.A.Brunt, 'The Roman Mob', *Past and Present* 35 (1966), 3-27 (repr. in M.I.Finley (ed.), *Studies in Ancient Society* (London, 1974), 74-102), who rightly takes seriously the grievances of those who offered their (sometimes violent) support to one or other leader.

21. The years 53 and 52 opened without consuls having yet been elected, and in the latter year Pompey was in the end elected sole consul—until he was joined by a colleague in the final month of the year. It was only with such power that he succeeded in putting an end to the activities of Publius Clodius, who (in our view) had started to create among his own supporters an alternative society in opposition to the state. (Compare here the 'alternative' way of life suggested by the poetry of Catullus—p. 23.)

increasingly complex society generated more and more areas of competition.[22]

But complexity had also its positive aspects. It not only provided more dynamite for self-destruction. The late Republic witnessed the beginnings of specialization and 'professionalism' in many areas of life that had not traditionally been defined or differentiated. We have already referred to the development of 'professional' poets (p. 20); let us also note the creation of a profession of specialized legal experts (but not of advocates or judges), the development of a specialized educational system, the emergence of technical experts in various areas of government. Many of these were to become more prominent in the new regime established by Augustus; but we should remember that the roots of the more 'differentiated' society of the empire lay in the late Republic. The changes in late Republican society should not be seen just as the causes of the breakdown of the specifically Republican political system; they were also parts of the *development* of Roman society, which underwent no clean break between the 'fall' of the Republic and the 'advent' of empire.[23]

22. Many of Cicero's speeches were delivered in defence of provincial governors; he also devoted a long letter (*To his Brother Quintus* 1, 1 (Shackleton Bailey 1)) to the pitfalls which a provincial governor needed to avoid.
23. See K.Hopkins, *Conquerors and Slaves*, 74-98. For the role of legal specialists, see above, p. 58.

Chapter Six

ROME AND THE OUTSIDE WORLD

The last century of the Republic saw both the final extension of Roman rule to the whole of the Mediterranean world and also the culmination of a process by which the society and economy of Italy were transformed out of all recognition. The two stories are intertwined and we have therefore decided to treat them in a single chapter, though both are large and complex.[1]

Roman imperialism

It is easy to be bemused by the success of Roman imperialism and by the sheer size of the Roman empire. As Polybius remarked already in the middle of the second century BC, the Romans had in effect conquered the known world in a couple of generations; and for us, who can observe the process in its entirety, the impression made is even stronger—and explanation is no easier. Indeed, more than with any other aspect of the Roman Republic, scholars dealing with the Roman acquisition of an empire have taken radically different views.[2]

Two particular explanations stand out among those which have been offered. On the one hand, there are those who claim, to put it crudely, that the whole Roman empire was acquired by accident or by a series of accidents; on the other, there are those who suggest that the Romans were consciously motivated in expanding their empire and were well aware of the profits they might gain from it. Here, as elsewhere, it may not be a question simply of one explanation being right and the other(s) being wrong. We do not necessarily have to make a choice; but we do need to consider both views more carefully in order to understand

1. The most accessible analysis of the interlocking aspects of Roman imperialism is that of Hopkins, *Conquerors and Slaves*, 1-74.
2. There is a good narrative account of the process of Roman expansion in R.M.Errington, *The Dawn of Empire* (London, 1971).

precisely how and why they differ, despite being founded on essentially the same body of evidence.

On one view, the Romans were not conscious imperialists, nor were they economically motivated. Their widespread conquests resulted from a series of defensive campaigns, mounted on behalf of themselves or their allies. This was indeed the opinion of the Romans themselves, who believed firmly that they only ever fought 'just wars'. So, for example, the outbreak of the Second Macedonian War (200-196), which made Rome the dominant power in the eastern Mediterranean, is seen as the result of the Roman fear of a potentially dangerous pact between Philip V of Macedonia and Antiochus III of Syria. Rome was generally successful in such allegedly defensive campaigns and so Roman territory expanded; but that expansion was not planned.[3]

This view does allow for a change in the nature of Roman imperialism in the very last period of the Republic after Sulla. The change is thought to involve a loss of scruple in Roman dealings with allies and subjects, as the Roman elite sought ever more territory to exploit and sought to exploit ever more fully the territory already held. But this process is seen principally as a feature of the corruption of government in the late Republic and not as something which requires explanation in the context of the development of the Roman empire.[4]

In opposition to the theory of defensive imperialism, it has recently been argued that the Romans consciously wanted, if not planned, to acquire overseas territory and that they were at least partly motivated by the desire for gain; however Roman conquests were justified at the time, self-defence was in fact only part of the story. This argument gives us a different perspective on the Second Macedonian War. Rome did not act just out of fear of her eastern rivals. The ambition and greed of individual politicians and of the Roman people as a whole were also important factors in the decision for war.[5]

This view also allows for a change in the nature of Roman imperialism in the latest phase of the Republic. In the period after Sulla, conquest came to be orchestrated not so much by the collective will of the Roman people, as by individuals. The Romans went on conquering;

---

3. Economic motivation for Roman expansion is most forcibly doubted by E.Badian, *Roman Imperialism*, 16-28; for the particular case of the Second Macedonian War, see A.H.McDonald and F.W.Walbank, 'The Origins of the Second Macedonian War', *JRS* 27 (1937), 180-207; more generally, see F.W.Walbank, 'Polybius and Rome's Eastern Policy', *JRS* 53 (1963), 1-13.
4. See Badian, *Roman Imperialism*, 61-92; *Publicans and Sinners*, 82-118.
5. The most important critique of traditional views is that of W.V.Harris, *War and Imperialism*, esp. 1-130, and 212-218 on the Second Macedonian War.

but now powerful men such as Pompey or Caesar, who effectively controlled much of the Mediterranean world for years on end, without reference to the senate or people, determined the process of conquest.[6]

The difference between these two opposing arguments lies essentially in their approach to the *motivation* of the Romans. The one suggests that the Romans acted for the reasons they themselves stated; the other that a defensive posture largely concealed less honourable motives: the desire for conquest, glory and profit.

The debate is not easy to resolve. Although the arguments for defensive imperialism seem to us—in any simple form—unsatisfactory, we should not imagine that the Romans were consistently insincere when they claimed that they had acted in defence of themselves and others. With hindsight, modern scholars can see a pattern of aggression; many members of the Roman elite, for much of the time, may have conceived of their own actions as defensive. We should also remember that much of the story is missing, namely what the Romans actually said and thought when they decided on acts of war—as distinct from the probably rationalised accounts of later historians. Such information would not provide the entire answer, but it would be a help. As it is, scholars are tempted to *infer* motives from the rather slender evidence of what the Romans actually did.

It is probably more fruitful, in fact, to discuss Roman imperialism in terms of the structures of Roman and Italian society, rather than the now irrecoverable motives of Roman politicians. Two factors are of particular significance. First, the pattern of Roman office-holding itself encouraged military expansion, since Roman magistrates, in their role as generals, traditionally had only one year to win the glory of a successful military campaign (pp. 55 and 69). A general could gain nothing for himself by deferring military action; for if it was put off to the next year, the prize of victory might fall to his successor. The competitive aspirations of the Roman elite thus encouraged year after year (consul after consul) the undertaking of wars that would give victory to the Roman people and prestige to their leaders. Secondly, Rome's system of dominance over her Italian allies also led to a high level of military activity and, with it, imperial expansion. For Rome demanded of the allies no yearly taxes in money or kind, but simply required that they provide troops for the Roman armies. Thus she had just one way to express her leadership in Italy: that is to make use of those troops (whose service she regarded as her due) by undertaking

6. See P.A.Brunt, 'Laus Imperii', in P.D.A.Garnsey and C.R.Whittaker (edd.), *Imperialism in the Ancient World* (Cambridge, 1978), 159-191, esp. 178-183.

further wars. Without military activity Rome's position as leader of Italy would not have been manifest. No doubt the burden of military service was at times resented by the allies (as taxation would have been); but as they too did well out of the wars their desire for gain provided a further factor encouraging wars of expansion.[7]

The debate over causes is not, however, the only issue, although it has tended to monopolise discussion of Roman imperialism. Let us now turn to consider some other important aspects of the development of Rome's empire which are often bypassed.

First, whatever the reasons for Roman expansion, Romans and Italians of all classes derived enormous benefits from the Roman empire. The elite, in particular senators, did specially well. But the societies of *publicani* also made fabulous fortunes. These societies, controlled by men of equestrian status, undertook the collection of taxes and other revenues from a number of provinces, often at great profit to themselves (p. 70); and they likewise profited by contracting for the erection of public buildings in Rome and Italy, buildings ultimately paid for by the provincial earnings of Rome (see pp. 13-14). Furthermore, a surplus of wealth in the hands of the elite stimulated production and trade, from which yet other groups below the top ranks of Roman and Italian society enriched themselves.[8]

Secondly, the Romans adopted at different times quite different approaches to the control of their conquests. In particular, the system they adopted in controlling their territory overseas was different from the one they had used in Italy. They normally organised their possessions overseas as provinces and controlled them through the presence of a magistrate and an army. In Italy, by contrast, as we shall see (pp. 77-80), their control of the peninsula had developed simply by concluding treaties with the different communities, after which the relationship was maintained by informal links between Roman aristocrats and their counterparts in the Italian cities.[9]

7. For the structural features underlying Roman imperialism see J.A.North, 'The Development of Roman Imperialism', *JRS* 71 (1981), 1-9; also, on the Italian dimension, A.D.Momigliano, *Alien Wisdom: the Limits of Hellenization* (Cambridge, 1975), 41-46. Competition to hold a triumph in the early second century BC is analysed by J.S.Richardson, 'The Triumph, the Praetors and the Senate', *JRS* 65 (1975), 50-63.
8. See J.S.Richardson, 'The Spanish Mines and the Development of Provincial Taxation in the Second Century BC', *JRS* 66 (1966), 139-152; There is a good account of the nature of the taxation and building contracts undertaken by the *publicani* in G.H.Stevenson, *Roman Provincial Administration till the Age of the Antonines* (Oxford, 1939), 142-144; M.H.Crawford, 'Rome and the Greek World: Economic Relationships', *Ec.Hist.Rev.* 30 (1977), 42-52, analyses the consequences for the Greek world of Roman exploitation.
9. A brief description of this important difference in the control of conquered territory

There were also long periods when the Romans did not *annex* territory and place it under their direct control, although they could in theory have done so. This might seem to show that the Romans were not systematic imperialists; but it is a mistake to confuse imperialism with annexation. The latter was only one of the ways in which it was possible to control overseas territory, even if it was common and, eventually, almost universal. Consider the period between the end of the third century and the middle of the second. Much is sometimes made of the fact that the Romans annexed no province between Spain at the beginning of that period and the territory of Carthage in 146; but the case of Macedonia suggests a different perspective. After the defeat of Perseus and the destruction of the Macedonian monarchy in 168-167, the country was divided into four so-called 'autonomous' regions. Yet these regions were just as much part of the Roman empire as if they had been formally annexed. They were, for example, subject to Roman taxation. It is not now entirely clear why in each case the Romans decided for or against direct annexation; but a specimen of the sort of reasoning which is likely to have gone on is preserved by the account in Strabo (63 BC-AD 21) of the Romans' reasons for not annexing Britain: it is suggested that the expense of controlling and governing Britain would be such that the net receipts from the province would be less than the revenues derived from customs dues on goods passing between Britain and the Roman Empire.[10]

Thirdly, the Roman Empire (although administered in a variety of different ways) acquired a coherent structure and logic of its own surprisingly quickly. In particular, despite its size and diversity, the empire came to form an economic unity, partly, it may be suggested, because of the system of taxation. For the taxes in money imposed by the Romans on conquered territory outside Italy forced the provincials to raise cash and thus to convert their surplus of agricultural produce into a form that could be more easily stored, transported and sold. These pressures encouraged trade, which linked together sometimes far distant parts of the empire; and at the same time, they encouraged

---

is given by Crawford, *Roman Republic*, 73, suggesting that treaties of *alliance* were almost entirely restricted to Italian communities from about 200.

10. The view we adopt here—that the Roman empire comprised any community which Rome effectively *dominated*—is very similar to that of Polybius. But note J.S.Richardson, 'Polybius' View of the Roman Empire', *PBSR* 34 (1979), 1-11, for the contrasting suggestion that the notion of a formally constituted *provincia* was central to the Romans' view of empire. He seems to us to overemphasize the 'un-Romanness' of Polybius' view. For Strabo on Britain, see *Geography* 2, 5, 8; 4, 5, 3.

urbanization, since towns provided, among other things, a convenient focus for exchange. The economic unity of the Mediterranean world came to be so firmly established that it survived the shock of the civil wars which eventually brought Augustus to power. We may speak loosely of the Roman world being shattered by these wars; in fact the empire did not fall apart.[11]

Finally, it is clear that the Romans, or at any rate some Romans, were aware of certain aspects of the complex relationship between the economy of central Italy, Italian and Roman society, Roman politics and the possession of an overseas empire, to which we have alluded (eg. p. 4); it is indeed an awareness of the problems posed by these complex relationships that lies behind the measures of the Gracchi and later reforming tribunes. Before *we* turn to analyse more fully the Italian aspect of these problems and to consider why the Italian allies of Rome rose in revolt in 91, it is necessary to look at the earlier, traditional structures of Rome's relationship with Italy.

Rome and Italy

Among the many factors which determined the pattern of Rome's relationship with Italy, we have chosen here to stress just three: the lack of a sharp division of status between Romans and their Italian allies; the internal political structures of Rome, which could readily incorporate as citizens men living far outside the city of Rome; and the co-operation of Romans and Italians in profitable imperial expansion. Each of these three factors contributed to the unity of Rome with Italy, a unity already evident at the time of the Second Punic War (218-201). For although Hannibal tried in the course of his invasion of Italy to revive Italian opposition to Rome (harking back to memories of Rome's *conquest* of the peninsula), he failed to gain decisive local support. Resistance to Rome, which had been virulent in the early stages of Roman expansion, in the fifth and fourth centuries BC, had largely died down by the third century BC.

An important element of diversity, paradoxically, underlay this unity. For, just as the Roman organisation of the empire overseas involved the use of a variety of methods of control, so Rome's conquest of Italy led to the existence of a mosaic of different types of community, with different privileges and statuses, both long established towns and newly

11. Our account here derives from K.Hopkins, 'Economic Growth in Towns in Classical Antiquity', in P.Abrams and E.A.Wrigley (ed.), *Towns in Societies* (Cambridge, 1978), 35-76; 'Taxes and Trade in the Roman Empire', *JRS* 70 (1980), 101-125.

founded towns, known as 'colonies'. There was no simple polarisation between privileged and unprivileged, no sharp distinction between Roman and Italian.

At one end of the spectrum, there was Rome and colonies in Italy founded by Rome, whose inhabitants enjoyed full Roman citizenship; then there were independent communities in the vicinity of Rome, the Latins—people descended, like the Romans, from the primitive Italian tribe of 'Latins'; then new Latin communities founded jointly by Rome and these other Latin cities, colonies founded by Rome alone with the status of a Latin community, Italian communities granted full Roman citizenship, Italian communities granted Roman citizenship without the right to vote, and finally allies with no 'Roman' rights at all. Though they were superficially fragmented, the cohesion of all these groups was encouraged because it was possible to pass from one status to another relatively easily; eventual access to Roman citizenship was in theory open to all. This Roman 'open-ness' was unique in the ancient world and contrasted strongly with the closed citizen bodies of the Greek *poleis* ('city-states').[12]

Secondly, the traditional structures of Roman political life allowed relatively easily the incorporation into the citizen body of far-flung outsiders, to which we have already alluded (p. 42). It might at first sight seem dangerously innovative that as a result of Roman expansion in Italy the rights and duties of Roman citizenship came eventually to be shared by people who did not live at or near Rome and probably never even came to the city. For this situation seems hard to reconcile with the character of Roman political institutions, which we have so far portrayed as those of a small urban community; and it is at sharp variance with the traditional pattern of the Greek *polis*, in which the urban centre and its territory round about were integrated at every level from that of cult to that of politics, and in which the direct participation in political life of the majority of the citizen body was assumed. Yet there are signs that Rome had never fitted that Greek model, even before her major period of expansion. For example, in the tribal assembly (see pp. 51-52), the very existence of four 'urban' tribes (*tribus* in Latin), voting groups of the population into which city dwellers exclusively were enrolled, and the progressive creation from the sixth century onwards of eventually 31 rural tribes suggest a clear and early separation of Rome from the surrounding countryside and

12. For a fuller account of the different types of community to be found in Italy, see Sherwin-White, *Citizenship*, 3-133 and 190-214; E.T.Salmon, *Roman Italy*, 40-72. There is a good short account in Jolowicz and Nicholas, *Roman Law*, 58-66.

an early assumption that citizenship could belong to those not officially resident in the city of Rome itself. Many changes occurred in
the course of the Republic: a smaller and smaller proportion of the
citizen body actually lived in or near Rome, as citizenship was granted
more widely in Italy and Roman citizens were planted in colonies in
often isolated parts of the peninsula; and conversely, from the third
century onwards the city of Rome swelled as it attracted considerable
Italian immigration. But despite such changes in detail, the pattern
of political organisation had long been set and it was not seriously
threatened—at least, not in the way the structures of a classical Greek
polis would have been—by the vast increase in size. The structure of
Rome's institutions could tolerate the addition of new territory and
new citizens far from Rome.[13]

The pattern of the Roman conquest of Italy meant that in most essential respects there came to be substantial uniformity in social and economic structure throughout Italy. On the eve of the Social War, in 91,
several languages other than Latin were still spoken in the peninsula,
and this linguistic diversity was no doubt matched by a continuing
sense that different Italian peoples in fact stemmed from different ethnic
groups. But the homogeneity of the country at this point was more
striking than its diversity. Roman roads linked most of the regions of
Italy; all of Italy used the same monetary system; men from all of Italy
served in the same armies in the conquest of the Mediterranean; they
joined in exploiting the lands which had been conquered. Moreover
the Italian governing classes were, like their Roman counterparts,
becoming increasingly 'Hellenized'. Many areas of Italy had of course
long been in contact with and borrowed from the Greek world independently of Rome. But by the first century, Rome was in effect the only
channel through which Greek influence reached Italy and it provided
a unifying focus for the cultural aspirations of the Italian upper classes:
as we have seen (p. 21), it was to Rome that writers flocked from all
over the peninsula in the age of Cicero.[14]

The homogeneity of Italy depended on two factors in particular.
First, strong links existed between the aristocracy of the city of Rome
and its local Italian counterparts. Secondly, among the people at large,
men from the city of Rome and men from the towns and countryside

13. The Roman tribal system is given its due place in the analysis of Finley, *Politics*,
84-92; there is a full account in L.R.Taylor, *The Voting Districts of the Roman Republic* (Papers
and Monographs, American Academy in Rome, 20, Rome, 1960).
14. For an account of the linguistic factor in two areas, see M.Pallottino, *The Etruscans*
(Harmondsworth, 1975), 189-208; E.T.Salmon, *Samnium and the Samnites* (Cambridge,
1967), 112-126.

of Italy gained tangible benefits from Roman expansion: booty and assignations of land; the chance to share in the plundering of the Mediterranean under the protection of Roman military might. So, for example, right up to the outbreak of the war in which the Italians demanded Roman citizenship, the Italian leaders were in continuous contact with members of the Roman governing class in the hope that they could persuade senate and assembly to grant citizenship of their own free will. And at about the same time, we find a clear indication that in the eastern Mediterranean Romans and Italians were regarded as *partners* in imperialism and exploitation. In 88, when the Roman province of Asia was invaded by King Mithridates VI of Pontus and Roman military protection proved inadequate, Romans and Italians were massacred together. Men from every part of Italy, resident in Asia as tax collectors, money-lenders or slave-traders, were all seen by the local inhabitants indifferently as *Romaioi*, Romans. The Italians, that is, did not appear as victims of Roman imperialism, but as beneficiaries of it.[15]

War with the allies

How then did it come about that in 91 Rome's Italian allies resorted to open warfare to gain full Roman citizenship? In what ways also did the problem of Rome's relationship with Italy add a further dimension to the agrarian problems faced by the Gracchi?

By the late second century BC, dangerous tensions had emerged between Romans and Italians, despite the traditional unifying structures that we have just described. On the one hand, access to full Roman citizenship became more difficult for the Italian allies, when (from the 160s) Rome ceased to found new settlements with the status of Latin colonies. These towns had previously formed in practice a half-way house to Roman citizenship; for Italian allies had usually been allowed to join such colonies and thus, as citizens of 'Latin' towns, they had the legal right to *Roman* citizenship if they chose to migrate to the city of Rome. When Latin colonies were no longer founded, that element of openness began to disappear. On the other hand, Rome became more assertive in the demands for manpower made on Italian

---

15. See Badian, *Foreign Clientelae*, 168-251, for an account of the relationship between Rome and Italy in this perspective; the emigration of men from Italy to exploit the different parts of the empire is discussed by A.J.N.Wilson, *Emigration from Italy in the Republican Age of Rome* (Manchester, 1966); Brunt, *Italian Manpower*, 158-265, esp. 224-227 for events in Asia in 88.

communities. For as Rome's own problems with military recruitment developed, the burden was increasingly shifted to the allies, who also, unlike Roman citizens after 167, paid taxes (to their local communities) to support the cost of the army contingents they supplied. The result was that the allies made sacrifice after sacrifice to create and preserve the Roman empire.[16]

Perhaps worst of all, the allies were debarred from any participation in the making of the decisions for which they had to fight. They were simply not members of the ruling people, with all the privileges that membership brought—protection, for example, against the (often arbitrary) demands of a Roman magistrate. The growing homogeneity of Italy and the standard assumption in the Greek world that the Italians *were* Romans, *Romaioi*, must have made this particularly bitter. One Latin community, the colony of Fregellae, felt so strongly about the oppressiveness of Roman rule that it revolted alone in 125, when a proposal which would have brought it citizenship was defeated in the assembly in Rome.[17]

Furthermore, in Italy as a whole, as well as in Roman territory, the poor had seen during the second century an ever greater proportion of the prizes of empire going to the elite. While the rich used the wealth they had gained from overseas conquest to acquire tracts of land in Italy, those outside the elite suffered from the end of the programme of colonization. For this halt did not simply mean the closure of one avenue to full Roman citizenship; it meant also an end to one of the principal economic rewards of victory, which had characterized the conquest of the further parts of the Italian peninsula by Rome and her allies: the precious allotment of land that for Romans and Italians alike went with membership of a Latin colony.

To make matters worse, the only action taken to remedy the agrarian problems (and the military problems that stemmed from them) related principally to Roman citizens alone. The solution of Tiberius Gracchus was (as we have seen) to make use of public land in order to settle those who had lost or had never possessed their own land. It is not certain whether or not Italians were entitled to benefit under the Gracchan law, but any entitlement which they did have was certainly inferior to that of Roman citizens. The allies were left with their

---

16. For the Roman use of Italian troops, see Brunt, *Italian Manpower*, 677-686.
17. For the revolt of Fregellae, see Stockton, *The Gracchi*, 96-98. For Italian aspirations in general, see the account of recent work in Sherwin-White, *Citizenship*, 134-149, 214-218; of particular importance are the articles of P.A.Brunt, 'Italian Aims at the Time of the Social War', *JRS* 55 (1965), 90-109, and Gabba, in *Republican Rome*, 70-130.

original burdens and with the same problems as Rome, but little hope of remedy.

The allies also sustained material losses. The measures of Tiberius and of his brother Caius Gracchus, ten years later, affected some Italian communities adversely. For Roman public land had traditionally been available for the use of these communities; and, no doubt, many of their richer members were among those (strictly speaking) illegal occupiers removed from their holdings to make way for Gracchan settlers. It was certainly these men who protested at the proposals to Tiberius Gracchus' cousin, Publius Scipio Aemilianus, using the normal channel of communication between Italy and Rome, that is personal contacts between local elites and the Roman elite. At the other end of the social scale, there is some evidence that the common Italian soldiers in the second century received less booty than their Roman counterparts.[18]

The effects of the processes we have described must have varied enormously from one Italian community to another and from one social level to another. But generally it is clear that, through the last decades of the second century, the Italians were becoming increasingly alienated from the Romans. In addition, tensions *within* the Italian communities themselves were increasing, just as they were at Rome; and these tensions no doubt played a part in alienating some communities (or some sections of some communities) even further from Rome. At the end, communication between Rome and Italy simply broke down: at Asculum, in Picenum, the Romans sent to urge restraint were murdered. War broke out.

Romanisation

Finally, let us turn to the Romanisation of Italy and the associated changes in Italian society during the first century BC, during the two generations which followed the war and the consequent grant of citizenship to most of the population of Italy.

Romanisation was not of course an entirely new phenomenon of the first century. Indeed it was already under way by the second century and, in part, lay behind the increasing tensions between Rome and Italy in the period before the outbreak of war in 91. It was not simply that the Romans became more oppressive in their demands on the

18. For Ti.Gracchus and the Italians, see J.S.Richardson, 'The Ownership of Roman Land. Tiberius Gracchus and the Italians', *JRS* 70 (1980), 1-11.

Italians—although that is certainly part of the story. An additional cause of Italian discontent was their increasing sense that they were as 'Roman' as the Romans, with the result that they felt resentful, if they were treated in any way as inferiors. Rome's success, that is, in incorporating her allies encouraged the latter to demand all the rights that they felt should go along with that incorporation.

But, in the two generations after the Social War, the level of Romanisation in Italy advanced yet further. This process can be clearly documented amongst the elite. More and more members of the newly enfranchised Italian aristocracies gained at least lower magistracies in the city of Rome; so that by the age of Augustus the Roman senate was full of men of Italian origin, many of whose descendants went on to hold the consulship. This pattern was traditional. For, on a smaller scale, throughout the history of the Republic families from communities newly granted Roman citizenship waited perhaps for a generation and then began their ascent to high office. And the avenues of advancement into the higher echelons of Roman society were also traditional: friendship with those already in power, wealth, oratorical skill, military expertise.[19]

It is more difficult to assess the Romanisation of the population of Italy as a whole. We can know very little of the culture and attitudes of individual members of the Italian poor—the illiterate farm labourer, for example, ignored by all our ancient literary sources. Yet, on a broader perspective, there are two indicators which can throw light on the survival, or submergence within Roman traditions, of distinctive local cultures in Italy: that is, language and religious or funerary practices.

The evidence of language is particularly striking. The northern part of Etruria, around Volaterrae or Arretium, was substantially untouched by Roman influence down to 91 BC. Use of the Etruscan language was universal, to judge from the evidence of inscriptions on stone; Latin remained an entirely 'foreign' tongue. In the generation after Sulla, however, bilingual inscriptions in Etruscan and Latin made their appearance and within the lifetime of Cicero, Etruscan virtually died out as a language inscribed on stone. A similar pattern is evident in the south, in Lucania, where, again to judge from inscriptions, Latin quickly became dominant in place of Oscan, the local language. At least at the level of the literate culture represented by these texts, regional variants were replaced by the uniformity of Latin.[20]

19. For paths of advancement for Italians, see Wiseman, *New Men*, 173-181.
20. See Salmon, *Roman Italy*, 152-157. For a bilingual (Latin—Etruscan) inscription, see *ILLRP* 904.

Funerary and religious practices allow us a glimpse of culture below
the level of literacy. The evidence for these is complex and often difficult
to interpret; but it seems to suggest again the emergence in the first
century BC of a relatively uniform set of customs throughout Italy.
Most clearly the archaeological evidence relating to funerary practices
consistently portrays the replacement of distinctive local practices, often
of great antiquity, by their standard Roman equivalents. Likewise with
religious and cultural diversity: different local calendars, incorporating a distinctive set of local religious festivals, seem to have died out,
as did also different local customs governing inheritance and
marriage.[21]

It remains to ask why the last generations of the Republic witnessed
such an enormous advance in Romanisation. The reason lies partly,
of course, with the longstanding tendency towards the unification of
Rome and Italy and the impetus given to that tendency by the
widespread grant of citizenship. But the tremendous speed with which
Romanisation advanced after Sulla was, in part, one of the side effects
of the turmoil of the late Republic. We have already discussed the pressure on Roman generals to provide land for their troops at the end
of campaigns. Let us consider this again from a different point of view.
Beginning in 59, with the veterans from the eastern wars of Pompey,
enormous numbers of men, who had been uprooted from their homes
and had served together for long periods, were settled in groups far
from their places of birth. The consequence was the shattering of the
existing social fabric both in their places of origin and in the communities in which they were settled. Once that fabric was shattered, the
increasingly dominant Roman culture became easily established all
over Italy. Paradoxically, one of the most lasting consequences of the
Roman Revolution was the homogeneous society of Italy from the age
of Augustus onwards.[22]

21. An example of a very distinctive type of local-style funerary monument, which dis-
appears by the age of Augustus may be found in M.W.Frederiksen, 'Republican Capua',
PBSR 27 (1959), 80-130.
22. See L.Keppie, *Colonisation and Veteran Settlement in Italy* (London, 1983); T.W.Potter,
The Changing Landscape of South Etruria (London, 1979), with the review of M.H.Craw-
ford in *Athenaeum* 59 (1980), 497-8.

Epilogue

Just as it is not easy to decide where to begin an account of the Roman revolution, so it is not obvious where to end it. No historian would dissent from the view that a Republican form of goverment was replaced by a monarchical form. But where should one place the transition?

Already in antiquity, different views were held. For Suetonius, Julius Caesar (who was assassinated in 44 BC) was the first of the Roman Emperors. For Appian, on the other hand, the civil wars which ushered in the Empire ended in 35, when Octavian, the future Emperor Augustus, returned to Rome, after eliminating all rivals but Mark Antony.[1] In a sense, of course, the question of a single turning point is an unreal one; the steps on the path to despotism were many.

In some ways, as we have seen, it makes sense to regard Pompey as the first *princeps*. Not only did he receive extravagant, almost monarchical, honours in the East (above, pp. 10-11), but some of his projects in Rome seem clear precursors of later 'imperial' projects. The elaborate architectural complex which he built, consisting of theatre, temple and spacious, colonnaded courtyards, resembles in the vastness of its conception not earlier building programmes by Republican magistrates, but the Forum of Caesar, or of Augustus, or of Trajan.[2] In other ways, Caesar *was* the first Emperor. After defeating Pompey in the Civil War of 49-48, he wielded practically autocratic power in Rome and enjoyed honours there greater than any of his Republican predecessors: he held the office of dictator, which was eventually granted to him as a *lifelong* position in February 44; he effectively controlled proceedings in the senate and the elections of magistrates; he held a religious position even in the city of Rome that was very close to out-right deification; he was attributed monarchical virtues such as *clementia* (clemency), desirable characteristics, that is, in a sole ruler, but entirely irrelevant to the traditional Roman aristocracy of equals. Although in many cases we can find precedents, somewhere in Roman history,

---

1. Note that Appian regarded the wars between 35 and the Battle of Actium in 31 BC not as civil, but as foreign ('Egyptian') war.
2. On Pompey's building projects, see (briefly) A.Boethius, *Etruscan and Early Roman Architecture* (rev. R.Ling and T.Rasmussen, Harmondsworth, 1978), 205-206; and (in greater detail) J.A.Hanson, *Roman Theater-Temples* (Princeton, 1959), 44-55.

for the individual honours which he received, his position as a whole was something quite different. He was like a king; and that was why he was murdered.[3]

Following Caesar, Octavian (his nephew and heir by adoption) was probably the first Roman to perceive, in the light of the career of his uncle, that sole rule was possible and to set out to achieve that end, by whatever means. Caesar had already gained power by civil war. But the violence which followed his death far surpassed all that had happened so far in brutality and horror. It lasted well over ten years, with different 'rounds' of conflict: between Mark Antony and Octavian; between Octavian (temporarily united with Antony) and the principal assassins of Caesar; between Octavian and the supporters of Antony, the younger son of Pompey and finally again Antony himself. It involved widespread proscription and murder, when Octavian and Antony together issued death warrants against over 300 senators (including Cicero) and some 2000 equestrians. It involved the dispossession of tens of thousands of Italian farmers, as vast numbers of veteran soldiers were settled on Italian land. When Octavian won the final victory against Antony at Actium in 31, his image must still have been that of a ruthless opportunist, not that of the judicious statesman—the first, 'good', emperor—with which we now (retrospectively) credit him.[4]

The 'Roman revolution' thus falls into two parts. The first—the fall of the Republic—we have discussed throughout this book. The second lies outside our present scope; for it consists in the process by which Octavian transformed himself—into the *princeps*, Augustus—and the Roman world—into that system we know as the Roman Empire. But the results of the Roman revolution, as a whole, are clear to see: the replacement of a 'Republic' by a monarchy; the emergence of a new governing class, drawing its recruits not only from the elite of Italy,

3. For a reliable narrative account of Caesar's career, see M.Gelzer, *Caesar* (Oxford, 1968) and, for discussion of the 'image' of Caesar, Z.Yavetz, *Julius Caesar and his Public Image* (London, 1983). The issue of his deification is fully discussed by S.Weinstock, *Divus Julius* (Oxford, 1971)—but note also the review by J.A.North, 'Praesens Divus', *JRS* 65 (1975), 171-177.
4. For an introductory narrative of this complicated 'triumviral' period, see J.M.Carter, *The Battle of Actium* (London, 1970). A very different view of the period (tending—unlike us—to stress its 'normality') is offered by F.G.B.Millar, 'Triumvirate and Principate', *JRS* 63 (1973), 50-67 (note that some of the important documents cited by Millar are now fully published in J.M.Reynolds, *Aphrodisias and Rome* (*JRS* Monographs 1, London, 1982), documents 7, 8, 10 and 12). The monarchical character of Augustus' regime is emphasized by F.G.B.Millar, 'State and Subject: the Impact of Monarchy', in F.G.B.Millar and E.Segal (edd.), *Caesar Augustus: Seven Aspects* (Oxford, 1984), 37-60.

but later from the Mediterranean as a whole; and, most important, after years of civil war, the construction of a new consensus in support of the new political order—an order which was regarded by Tacitus, a century later, as a bitter necessity.

Appendix:
Literary sources in translation

Translations of all the ancient sources we have referred to in the text or notes are available (with the minor exceptions mentioned below) in the Loeb Classical Library. We have, therefore, chosen to list here only those works not available in Loeb translation, those oddly classified (and so difficult to locate) in the Loeb Classical Library and some of those for which other good translations are readily available.

Section A includes works of Republican authors contemporary with the period we have been discussing. Section B comprises works of ancient authors writing after that period. Although written in Latin or Greek, these works should not be regarded as *primary* sources in the strictest sense. After all, Plutarch, for example, was writing 200 years after the death of Tiberius Gracchus.

Section A

Caesar: *The Battle for Gaul, a new translation* tr. A.and P.Wiseman (London, 1980).
  The Conquest of Gaul (Penguin Classics).
Catullus: *The Poems* (Penguin Classics).
  Catullus: tr. G.P.Goold (London, 1983).
Cicero: *Letters to Atticus*, *Letters to his Friends*, *Letters to his Brother Quintus*. For all the letters of Cicero the translations of D.R.Shackleton Bailey (available in Penguin Classics) are particulary recommended. We have indicated in our references to the letters both the standard numbering of the texts (used by the Loeb translation) and the new numbering of Shackleton Bailey.
  Selected Political Speeches (Penguin Classics) includes *On the Command of Cn. Pompeius*, *Against Lucius Sergius Catilina*, *In Defence of the Poet Aulus Licinius Archias* and *The First Philippic against Marcus Antonius*.
  Selected Works (Penguin Classics) includes *The Second Philippic*, *Against Verres* 1 and *On Duties* 3.
  On the Good Life (Penguin Classics) includes *On Duties* 2.

On Moral Obligation (= *On Duties*), tr. J.Higginbotham (London, 1967).

The Nature of the Gods (Penguin Classics).

On the Commonwealth (= *On the Republic*), tr. G.H.Sabine and S.B.Smith (Columbus, Ohio, 1929).

Q. Cicero: *A Short Guide to Electioneering*, tr. D.W.Taylor and J.Murrell (Lactor 3, London, 1968). (The Loeb translation of this work is included in the fourth volume of Cicero's *Letters to Friends*).

Ennius: in Loeb, *Remains of Old Latin* 1.

Livius Andronicus: in Loeb, *Remains of Old Latin* 2.

Lucilius: in Loeb, *Remains of Old Latin* 3.

Lucretius: *On the Nature of the Universe* (Penguin Classics).

On Nature, tr. R.M.Geer (The Library of Liberal Arts, Indianapolis etc., 1965).

On the Nature of Things, tr. M.F.Smith (London, 1965).

Pacuvius: in Loeb, *Remains of Old Latin* 2.

Plautus: *The Rope and Other Plays* (= *The Ghost, A Three-Dollar Day, Amphitryo*) (Penguin Classics).

A Pot of Gold and Other Plays (= *The Prisoners, The Brothers Menaechmus, The Swaggering Soldier, Pseudolus*) (Penguin Classics).

Polybius: *The Rise of the Roman Empire* (= Selections of *The Histories*) (Penguin Classics).

Sallust: *Jugurthine War and Conspiracy of Catiline* (Penguin Classics).

Terence: *The Comedies* (Penguin Classics).

The Comedies of Terence, tr. F.O.Copley (The Library of Liberal Arts, Indianapolis etc., 1967).

There is no convenient translation of the fragments of Q.Fabius Pictor, L.Cincius Alimentus, Cato's *Origines* or Asinius Pollio. The original Latin texts (or Greek in the case of Pictor) may be found in H.Peter, *Historicorum Romanorum Reliquiae* (Leipzig, 1906). The fragments of Panaetius (not translated) are collected in *Panaetii Rhodii Fragmenta*, ed. M.Van Straaten (Leiden, 1962).

Section B

Augustus: *Res Gestae Divi Augusti: the Achievements of the Divine Augustus*, tr. P.A.Brunt and J.M.Moore (Oxford, 1967).

Note that, in the Loeb Classical Library, the translation of the *Res Gestae* is appended to the translation of the *Histories* of Velleius

Paterculus.

Gaius: *The Institutes* tr. F.De Zulueta (Oxford, 1946). (There is no Loeb
translation of this work.)

Livy: *The Early History of Rome* (= *History of Rome* 1-5) (Penguin Classics).
Rome and Italy (= *History of Rome* 6-10) (Penguin Classics).
The War with Hannibal (= *History of Rome* 21-30) (Penguin Classics).
Rome and the Mediterranean (= *History of Rome* 31-45) (Penguin Classics).

Plutarch: *Fall of the Roman Republic* (Penguin Classics), includes the *Lives
of Marius, Sulla, Crassus, Pompey, Caesar and Cicero.*

Suetonius: *The Twelve Caesars* (Penguin Classics).

Anthologies

Note the following collections of sources:

From the Gracchi to Sulla. Sources for Roman History, 133—80 BC, tr. D.
Stockton (Lactor 13, London, 1981).

W.K.Lacey and B.W.J.G.Wilson, *Res Publica: Roman Politics and Society
according to Cicero* (Bristol,1978).

N.Lewis and M.Reinhold, *Roman Civilization,* vol. 1, *The Republic* (New
York, 1951).

There is no convenient translation of the *Facta et Dicta Memorabilia (Anecdotes)* of Valerius Maximus. The original Latin text may be found in
the edition of C.Kempf (Leipzig, 1888).

Bibliography and abbreviations

AJA	*American Journal of Archaeology*
AJPh	*American Journal of Philology*
ANRW	*Aufstieg und Niedergang der Römischen Welt* (Berlin and New York).
Bull.J.Ryl.Lib.	*Bulletin of the John Rylands Library*
Coll. Lat.	Collection Latomus
CQ	*Classical Quarterly*
CSSH	*Comparative Studies in Society and History*
DdA	*Dialoghi di Archeologia*
Ec.Hist.Rev.	*Economic History Review*
G&R	*Greece and Rome*
ILLRP	*Inscriptiones Latinae Liberae Rei Publicae* (ed A. Degrassi) (2 vols, Florence, 1957, 1963)
ILLRP Imagines	*Inscriptiones Latinae Liberae Rei Publicae, Imagines* (ed. A.Degrassi) (Berlin, 1965) — illustrations of inscriptions
JRS	*Journal of Roman Studies*
PBSR	*Papers of the British School at Rome*
PCPhS	*Proceedings of the Cambridge Philological Society*
TAPhA	*Transactions of the American Philological Association*
YClS	*Yale Classical Studies*
ZPE	*Zeitschrift für Papyrologie und Epigraphik*

	W.G.Arnott, *Menander, Plautus, Terence* (*Greece and Rome* New Survey, 9, Oxford, 1975).
	A.E.Astin, *The Lex Annalis before Sulla* (Coll.Lat. 32, Brussels, 1958).
	A.E.Astin, 'Leges Aelia et Fufia', *Latomus* 23 (1964), 421-445.
Astin, *Scipio*	A.E.Astin, *Scipio Aemilianus* (Oxford, 1967).
Astin, *Cato*	A.E.Astin, *Cato the Censor* (Oxford, 1978).
	R.F.Atkinson, *Knowledge and Explanation in History: an introduction to the Philosophy of History* (London, 1978).
	M.M.Austin and P.Vidal Naquet, *Economic and Social History of Ancient Greece* (London, 1977).
	E.Badian, 'Lex Acilia Repetundarum', *AJPh* 75 (1954), 374-384.
Badian, *Foreign Clientelae*	E.Badian, *Foreign Clientelae (264-70BC)* (Oxford, 1958).

E.Badian, 'Caesar's *Cursus* and the Intervals between Offices', *JRS* 49 (1959), 81-89 (repr. in Badian, *Studies*, 140-156).

Badian, 'Gracchi to Sulla'   E.Badian, 'From the Gracchi to Sulla (1940-1959)', *Historia* 11 (1962), 197-245 (repr. in Seager, *Crisis*, 3-51).

E.Badian, 'Waiting for Sulla', *JRS* 52 (1962), 47-61 (repr. in Badian, *Studies*, 206-234).

Badian, *Studies*   E.Badian, *Studies in Greek and Roman History* (Oxford, 1964).

Badian, 'Early Historians'   E.Badian, 'The Early Historians', in T.A.Dorey (ed.), *Latin Historians* (London, 1966), 1-38.

Badian, *Roman Imperialism*   E.Badian, *Roman Imperialism in the Late Republic* (2nd ed., Oxford, 1968).

E.Badian, *Lucius Sulla: the Deadly Reformer* (Sydney, 1970).

Badian, *Publicans and Sinners*   E.Badian, *Publicans and Sinners* (Oxford, 1972).

E.Badian, 'Tiberius Gracchus and the Beginning of the Roman Revolution', *ANRW* 1, 1 (1972), 668-731.

E. Badian, 'The Silence of Norbanus: a Note on Provincial Quaestors under the Republic', *AJPh* 104 (1983), 156-171.

J.P.V.D.Balsdon, 'The History of the Extortion Court at Rome, 123-70 BC', *PBSR* 14 (1938) 98-114 (repr. in Seager, *Crisis*, 132-148).

J.P.V.D.Balsdon, 'Sulla Felix', *JRS* 41 (1951), 1-10.

J.P.V.D.Balsdon, 'Roman History, 58-56 BC: three Ciceronian problems', *JRS* 47 (1957), 15-20.

J.P.V.D.Balsdon, 'Fabula Clodiana', *Historia* 15 (1966), 65-73.

Banton, *Anthropological Approaches*   M.Banton (ed), *Anthropological Approaches to the Study of Religion* (ASA Monographs, 3, London, 1966).

C.Belsey, *Critical Practice* (London, 1980).

Bianchi Bandinelli, *Rome*   R.Bianchi Bandinelli, *Rome: the Centre of Power* (London, 1970).

R.Bloch, *The Origins of Rome* (London, 1960).

A.Boethius, *Etruscan and Early Roman Architecture* (rev. R.Ling and T.Rasmussen, Harmondsworth, 1978).

S.F.Bonner, *Education in Ancient Rome* (London, 1977).

G.W.Bowersock, *Augustus and the Greek World* (Oxford, 1965).

G.K.Boyce, *Corpus of the Lararia of Pompeii (Memoirs*

of the American Academy at Rome 14, 1937).

J.C.Bramble, 'Structure and Ambiguity in Catullus 64', *PCPhS* 16 (1970), 22-41.

T.R.S.Broughton, *The Magistrates of the Roman Republic,* 2 vols (New York, 1951, 1952).

Brunt, 'The Army and the Land'
P.A.Brunt, 'The Army and the Land in the Roman Revolution', *JRS* 52 (1962), 69-86.

P.A.Brunt, '*Amicitia* in the Late Roman Republic', *PCPhS* 11 (1965), 1-20 (repr. in Seager, *Crisis,* 199-218).

P.A.Brunt, 'Italian Aims at the Time of the Social War', *JRS* 55 (1965), 90-109.

Brunt, 'Equites'
P.A.Brunt, 'The Equites in the Late Republic', in *Trade and Politics in the Ancient World* (2nd International Conference of Economic History, 1962: Paris, The Hague, 1965), 117-149 (repr. in Seager, *Crisis,* 83-115).

P.A.Brunt, review of Earl, *Tiberius Gracchus, Gnomon* 37 (1965), 189-192.

P.A.Brunt, 'The Roman Mob', *Past and Present* 35 (1966), 3-27 (repr. in M.I.Finley (ed.), *Studies in Ancient Society* (London, 1974), 74-102.

P.A.Brunt, Review of Ch. Meier, *Res Publica Amissa* (Wiesbaden, 1966), *JRS* 58 (1968), 229-232.

Brunt, *Italian Manpower*
P.A.Brunt, *Italian Manpower, 225 BC—AD 14* (Oxford, 1971).

Brunt, *Social Conflicts*
P.A.Brunt, *Social Conflicts in the Roman Republic* (London, 1971).

P.A.Brunt, 'Two Great Roman Landowners', *Latomus* 34 (1975), 619-635.

P.A.Brunt, 'Laus Imperii', in P.D.A.Garnsey and C.R.Whittaker (edd.), *Imperialism in the Ancient World* (Cambridge, 1978), 159-191.

Brunt, '*Nobilitas* and *Novitas*'
P.A.Brunt, '*Nobilitas* and *Novitas*', *JRS* 72 (1982), 1-17.

Cambridge Ancient History 10
The Cambridge Ancient History, vol. 10, *The Augustan Empire, 44 BC—AD 70* (Cambridge, 1952).

Cambridge History of Classical Literature, 2
The Cambridge History of Classical Literature: 2, Latin Literature (edd. E.J.Kenney and W.V.Clausen, Cambridge, 1982).

J.M.Carter, *The Battle of Actium* (London, 1970).

Civiltà del Lazio Primitivo (Exhibition Catalogue, Rome, 1976).

F.Coarelli, 'Public Building in Rome between the Second Punic War and the Death of Sulla', *PBSR* 32 (1977), 1-23

M.Coffey, *Roman Satire* (London and New York, 1976).

T.J.Cornell, 'Review of Wiseman, *Clio's Cosmetics*', *JRS* 72 (1982), 203-206.

T.J.Cornell and J.Matthews, *Atlas of the Roman World* (Oxford, 1982).

M.H.Crawford, *Roman Republican Coinage* (Cambridge, 1974).

M.H.Crawford, 'Hamlet without the Prince' (review of Gruen, *Last Generation*), *JRS* 66 (1976), 214-217.

M.H.Crawford, 'Rome and the Greek World: Economic Relationships', *Ec.Hist.Rev.* 30 (1977), 42-52.

Crawford, *Roman Republic*   M.H.Crawford, *The Roman Republic* (London, 1978).

M.H.Crawford, Review of T.W.Potter, *The Changing Landscape of South Etruria* (London, 1979), *Athenaeum* 59 (1980), 497-498.

J.A.Crook, *Consilium Principis* (Cambridge, 1955).

Crook, *Law and Life*   J.A.Crook, *Law and Life of Rome* (London, 1967).

L.C.Curran, 'Catullus 64 and the Heroic Age', *YClS* 21 (1969), 171-192.

L.W.Daly, 'Roman Study Abroad', *AJPh* 71 (1950), 40-58.

J.H.D'Arms, *Commerce and Social Standing in Ancient Rome* (Cambridge, Mass. and London, 1981).

R.Develin, *Patterns in Office Holding, 366 — 49 BC* (Coll. Lat. 161, Brussels, 1979).

A.E.Douglas, *Cicero* (*Greece and Rome* New Survey 2, Oxford, 1968).

Dumézil, *Archaic Roman Religion*   G.Dumézil, *Archaic Roman Religion* (Chicago and London, 1970).

Earl, *Tiberius Gracchus*   D.C.Earl, *Tiberius Gracchus: a Study in Politics* (Coll. Lat. 66, Brussels, 1963).

Earl, *Political Tradition*   D.C.Earl, *The Moral and Political Tradition of Rome* (London, 1967).

Enea nel Lazio: archeologia e mito (Exhibition Catalogue, Rome, 1981).

R.M.Errington, *The Dawn of Empire* (London, 1971).

E.E.Evans-Pritchard, *Nuer Religion* (Oxford, 1956).

E.E.Evans-Pritchard, *Theories of Primitive Religion* (Oxford, 1965).

E.E.Evans-Pritchard, *Witchcraft, Oracles and Magic among the Azande* (Oxford, 1976).

B.Farrington, *Science and Politics in the Ancient World*

(London, 1939).

B.Farrington, 'Form and Purpose in the *De Rerum Natura*' in D.R.Dudley (ed.), *Lucretius* (London, 1965), 19-34.

M.I.Finley (ed.), *Slavery in Classical Antiquity* (Cambridge, 1960).

M.I.Finley, 'The Silent Women of Rome', in *Aspects of Antiquity* (London, 1981), 129-142.

M.I.Finley, *The Ancient Economy* (London, 1973).

M.I.Finley, 'The Ancient City from Fustel de Coulanges to Max Weber and beyond', *CSSH* 19 (1977), 305-327 (repr. in Finley, *Economy and Society*, 3-23).

M.I.Finley, *Ancient Slavery and Modern Ideology* (London, 1980).

Finley, *Economy and Society*   M.I.Finley, *Economy and Society in Ancient Greece* (B.D.Shaw and R.P.Saller (edd.), London, 1981).

Finley, *Politics*   M.I.Finley, *Politics in the Ancient World* (Cambridge, 1983).

M.W.Frederiksen, 'The Contribution of Archaeology to the Agrarian Problem in the Gracchan Period' , *DdA* 4-5 (1970-71), 330-367.

M.W.Frederiksen, 'Republican Capua', *PBSR* 14, (1959), 80-130.

From the Gracchi to Sulla. Sources for Roman History, 133—80 BC, translated by D.Stockton (LACTOR 13, London, 1981).

A.C.Frothingham, 'Ancient Orientation Unveiled: 2, Etruria and Rome', *AJA* 21 (1917), 187-201.

Gabba, *Republican Rome*   E.Gabba, *Republican Rome, the Army and the Allies* (Oxford, 1976).

E.Gabba, Review of Nicolet, *World of the Citizen*, *JRS* 67 (1977), 192-194.

E.Gabba, 'The Historians and Augustus', in F.G.B.Millar and E.Segal (edd.), *Caesar Augustus: seven aspects* (Oxford, 1984), 61-88.

P.D.A.Garnsey, 'Peasants in Ancient Roman Society', *Journal of Peasant Studies* 3 (1976), 221-235.

L.Gatti lo Guzzo, *Il deposito votivo dall'Esquilino detto di Minerva Medica* (Studi e materiali di etruscologia e antichità Italiche, 17, Rome, 1978).

M.Gelzer, *Caesar* (Oxford, 1968).

Gelzer, *Roman Nobility*   M.Gelzer, *The Roman Nobility* (Oxford, 1969).

R.J.Goar, *Cicero and the State Religion* (Amsterdam, 1972).

R.L.Gordon, 'Mithraism and Roman Society:

social factors in the explanation of religious change', *Religion* 2,2 (1972), 92-121.

Greenidge, *Roman Public Life*
A.J.Greenidge, *Roman Public Life* (London, 1901).

A.J.Greenidge, *The Legal Procedure of Cicero's Time* (Oxford, 1901; repr. New York 1971).

E.S.Gruen, 'P. Clodius Pulcher, Instrument or Independent Agent?' *Phoenix* 20 (1966), 120-130.

E.S.Gruen, *Roman Politics and the Roman Criminal Courts, 149 BC—78 BC* (Cambridge, Mass., 1968).

Gruen, *Last Generation*
E.S.Gruen, *The Last Generation of the Roman Republic* (Berkeley, etc, 1974).

D.E.Hahm, 'Roman Nobility and the Three Major Priesthoods, 218-167 BC' *TAPhA* 94 (1963), 73-85.

J.A.Hanson, *Roman Theater-Temples* (Princeton, 1959).

E.G.Hardy, *The Catilinarian Conspiracy in its Context: a Re-study of the Evidence* (Oxford, 1924).

W.V.Harris, 'The Development of the Quaestorship, 267-81 BC', *CQ* 26 (1976), 92-106.

Harris, *War and Imperialism*
W.V.Harris, *War and Imperialism in Republican Rome, 327—70 BC* (Oxford, 1979).

W.V.Harris, 'Literacy and Epigraphy 1', *ZPE* 52 (1983), 87-111.

J.R.Hawthorn, 'The Senate after Sulla', *G&R* 9 (1962), 53-60.

U.M.Heibges, 'Religion and Rhetoric in Cicero's Speeches', *Latomus* 28 (1969), 833-849.

U.W.Hiesinger, 'Portraiture in the Roman Republic', *ANRW* 1, 4 (1973), 805-825.

Hopkins, *Conquerors and Slaves*
K.Hopkins, *Conquerors and Slaves* (Sociological Studies in Roman History, 1, Cambridge, 1978).

K.Hopkins, 'Economic Growth in Towns in Classical Antiquity', in P.Abrams and E.A.Wrigley (edd.), *Towns in Societies* (Cambridge, 1978), 35-76.

K.Hopkins, 'Taxes and Trade in the Roman Empire', *JRS* 70 (1980), 101-125.

Hopkins, *Death and Renewal*
K.Hopkins, *Death and Renewal* (Sociological Studies in Roman History, 2, Cambridge, 1983).

S.C.Humphreys, *Anthropology and the Greeks* (London, 1978).

W.F.Jashemski, *The Origins and History of the Proconsular and Propraetorian Imperium* (Chicago, 1950).

H.D.Jocelyn, 'The Roman Nobility and the

Religion of the Roman State', *Journal of Religious History* 4 (1966), 89-104.

Jolowicz and Nicholas, *Roman Law* — H.F.Jolowicz and B.Nicholas, *Historical Introduction to the Study of Roman Law* (Cambridge, 1972).

D.K.Jordan, *Gods, Ghosts and Ancestors: the folk religion of a Taiwanese village* (Berkeley, 1972).

A.H.M.Jones, 'Taxation in Antiquity', in *The Roman Economy* (Oxford, 1974), 151-186.

J.M.Kelly, *Roman Litigation* (Oxford, 1968).

G.Kennedy, *The Art of Rhetoric in the Roman World* (Princeton, 1972).

E.J.Kenney, *Lucretius* (*Greece and Rome* New Survey 11, Oxford, 1977).

L.Keppie, *Colonisation and Veteran Settlement in Italy* (London, 1983).

L.Keppie, *The Making of the Roman Army: from Republic to Empire* (London, 1984).

W.K.Lacey, 'The Tribunate of Curio', *Historia* 10 (1961), 318-329.

W.K.Lacey, *Cicero and the End of the Roman Republic* (London, etc., 1978).

J.Leach, *Pompey the Great* (London, 1978).

M.R.Lefkowitz and M.B.Fant, *Women's Life in Greece and Rome: a Sourcebook in Translation* (London, 1982).

Liebeschuetz, *Continuity and Change* — J.H.W.G.Liebeschuetz, *Continuity and Change in Roman Religion* (Oxford, 1979).

J.Linderski, 'Constitutional Aspects of the Consular Elections in 59 BC', *Historia* 14 (1965), 423-442.

A.W.Lintott, 'P. Clodius Pulcher—*Felix Catilina?*', *G&R* 14 (1967), 157-169.

Lintott, *Violence* — A.W.Lintott, *Violence in Republican Rome* (Oxford, 1968).

A.W.Lintott, 'Provocatio: from the Struggle of the Orders to the Principate', *ANRW* 1, 2 (1972), 226-267.

A.W.Lintott, 'Cicero and Milo', *JRS* 64 (1974), 62-78.

Loewenstein, *Governance of Rome* — K.Loewenstein, *The Governance of Rome* (The Hague, 1973).

R.O.A.M.Lyne, *The Latin Love Poets* (Oxford, 1980).

B.MacBain, *Prodigy and Expiation: a Study in Religion and Politics in Republican Rome* (Coll.Lat.177, Brussels, 1982).

A.H.McDonald and F.W.Walbank, 'The Origins of the Second Macedonian War', *JRS* 27 (1937), 180-207.

A.MacIntyre, 'The Idea of a Social Science', in B.R.Wilson (ed.), *Rationality* (Oxford, 1970), 112-130.

R.MacMullen, *Roman Social Relations* (Newhaven and London, 1974).

A.J.Marshall, 'Library Resources and Creative Writing at Rome', *Phoenix* 30 (1976), 252-264.

R.Mellor, *Thea Rome: the Worship of the Goddess Roma in the Greek World* (Hypomnemata 42, Göttingen, 1975).

Michigan Papyri 3 (Ann Arbor, 1936).

F.G.B.Millar, 'Triumvirate and Principate', *JRS* 63 (1973), 50-67.

F.G.B.Millar, *The Emperor in the Roman World* (London, 1977).

F.G.B.Millar, 'The Political Character of the Classical Roman Republic, 200-151 BC', *JRS* 74 (1984), 1-19.

F.G.B.Millar, 'State and Subject: the Impact of Monarchy', in F.G.B.Millar and E.Segal (edd.), *Caesar Augustus: Seven Aspects* (Oxford, 1984), 37-60.

A.D.Momigliano, 'Perizonius, Niebuhr and the Character of Early Roman Tradition', *JRS* 47 (1957), 104-114 (repr. in *Essays in Ancient and Modern Historiography* (Oxford, 1977), 231-251).

A.D.Momigliano, *Alien Wisdom: the Limits of Hellenization* (London, 1975).

J.M.Moore, *Aristotle and Xenophon on Democracy and Oligarchy* (2nd. ed., London, 1982).

M.G.Morgan, 'The Portico of Metellus: a reconsideration', *Hermes* 99 (1971), 9480-505.

Mysteries of Diana: the Antiquities from Nemi in Nottingham Museums (Castle Museum, Nottingham, 1983).

D.B.Nagle, 'The Failure of the Roman Political Process in 133 BC', *Athenaeum* 48 (1970) , 372-394; 49 (1971), 111-128.

J.K.Newman, *Augustus and the New Poetry* (Coll. Lat. 88, Burssels, 1976).

Nicolet, *World of the Citizen*   C.Nicolet, *The World of the Citizen in Republican Rome* (London, 1980).

W.Nippel, 'Policing Rome', *JRS* 74 (1984), 20-29.

J.A.North, 'Praesens Divus' (review of S.Weinstock,

Divus Julius (Oxford, 1971)), *JRS* 65 (1975), 171-177.

North, 'Conservatism and Change'
J.A.North, 'Conservatism and Change in Roman Religion', *PBSR* 44 (1976), 1-12.

J.A.North, 'Religious Toleration in Republican Rome', *PCPhS* 25 (1979), 85-103.

J.A.North, 'Novelty and Choice in Roman Religion', *JRS* 70 (1980), 186-191.

J.A.North, 'The Development of Roman Imperialism', *JRS* 71 (1981), 1-9.

Ogilvie, *Romans and their Gods*
R.M.Ogilvie, *The Romans and their Gods* (London, 1969).

R.M.Ogilvie, *Roman Literature and Society* (Harmondsworth, 1980).

M.Pallottino, *The Etruscans* (Harmondsworth, 1975).

P.Pensabene et al., *Terracotte votive dal Tevere* (Studi Miscellanei 25, Rome, 1980).

J.J.Pollitt, 'The Impact of Greek Art on Rome', *TAPhA* 108 (1978), 155-174.

Pollitt, *Art of Rome*
J.J.Pollitt, *The Art of Rome c753 BC—AD 337: Sources and Documents* (Cambridge, 1983).

S.B.Pomeroy, *Goddesses, Whores, Wives and Slaves* (London, 1976).

T.W.Potter, *The Changing Landscape of South Etruria* (London, 1979).

Prima Italia: arts Italiques du premier millénaire avant J.C. (Brussels, 1980 = Rome, 1981).

D.W.Rathbone, 'The Development of Agriculture in the Ager Cosanus during the Roman Republic: Problems of Evidence and Interpretation', *JRS* 71 (1981), 10-23.

D.W.Rathbone, 'The Slave Mode of Production in Italy', *JRS* 73 (1983), 160-168.

E.D.Rawson, 'The Interpretation of Cicero's *De Legibus*', *ANRW* 1, 4 (1973), 334-356.

E.D.Rawson, 'Scipio, Laelius, Furius and the Ancestral Religion', *JRS* 63 (1973), 161-174.

E.D.Rawson, 'Architecture and Sculpture: the Activities of the Cossutii', *PBSR* 30 (1975), 36-47.

Rawson, *Cicero*
E.D.Rawson, *Cicero: a Portrait* (London, 1975).

E.D.Rawson, 'The Introduction of Logical Organisation in Roman Prose Literature', *PBSR* 33 (1978), 12-34

E.D.Rawson, *Intellectual Life in the Late Roman*

Republic (London, forthcoming).

J.M.Reynolds, *Aphrodisias and Rome* (*JRS* Monographs 1, London, 1982).

J.W.Rich, 'The Supposed Roman Manpower Shortage of the Later Second Century BC', *Historia* 32 (1983), 287-331.

J.S.Richardson, 'The Spanish Mines and the Development of Provincial Taxation in the Second Century BC', *JRS* 66 (1976), 139-152.

J.S.Richardson, 'The *Commentariolum Petitionis*', *Historia* 20 (1971), 436-442.

J.S.Richardson, 'The Triumph, the Praetors and the Senate', *JRS* 65 (1975), 50-63.

J.S.Richardson, *Roman Provincial Administration, 227 BC—AD 117* (London, 1976).

J.S.Richardson, 'Polybius' View of the Roman Empire', *PBSR* 34 (1979), 1-11.

J.S.Richardson, 'The Ownership of Roman Land: Tiberius Gracchus and the Italians', *JRS* 70 (1980), 1-11.

R.T.Ridley, 'The Extraordinary Commands of the Late Republic: a Problem of Definition', *Historia* 30 (1981), 280-297.

H.J.Rose, *A Handbook of Latin Literature* (3rd ed., London, 1954).

R.P.Saller, 'Anecdotes as Historical Evidence for the Principate', *G&R* 27 (1980), 69-83.

E.T.Salmon, *Samnium and the Samnites* (Cambridge, 1967).

E.T.Salmon, *Roman Colonisation under the Republic* (London, 1969).

Salmon, *Roman Italy*   E.T.Salmon, *The Making of Roman Italy* (London, 1982).

F.H.Sandbach, *The Comic Theatre of Greece and Rome* (London, 1977).

F.Schulz, *History of Roman Legal Science* (Oxford, 1946).

H.H.Scullard, *Scipio Africanus: Soldier and Politician* (London, 1970).

H.H.Scullard, *Roman Politics, 220-150 BC* (2nd ed., Oxford, 1973).

Scullard, *Festivals*   H.H.Scullard, *Festivals and Ceremonies of the Roman Republic* (London, 1981).

Scullard, *Gracchi to Nero*   H.H.Scullard, *From the Gracchi to Nero* (5th ed., London, 1982).

Seager, *Crisis*   R.Seager (ed.), *The Crisis of the Roman Republic* (Cambridge and New York, 1969).

R.Seager, 'Factio', *JRS* 62 (1972), 53-58.

R.Seager, 'Cicero and the Word *Popularis*', *CQ* 22 (1972), 328-338.

D.R.Shackleton Bailey, 'The Roman Nobility in the Second Civil War', *CQ* 10 (1960), 253-267.

I.Shatzman, *Senatorial Wealth and Roman Politics* (Coll. Lat. 142, Brussels, 1975).

A.N.Sherwin-White, 'Violence in Roman Politics', *JRS* 46 (1956), 1-9 (repr. in Seager, *Crisis*, 151-159).

Sherwin-White, *Citizenship* A.N.Sherwin-White, *The Roman Citizenship* (2nd ed., Oxford, 1973).

A.N.Sherwin-White, 'The Lex Repetundarum and the Political Ideas of Gaius Gracchus', *JRS* 72 (1982), 18-31.

R.E.Smith, *Service in the Post-Marian Roman Army* (Manchester, 1958).

Smith, 'Portraiture' R.R.R.Smith, 'Greeks, Foreigners and Roman Republican Portraiture', *JRS* 71 (1981), 24-38.

W.Smith, etc., *A Dictionary of Greek and Roman Antiquities* vol. 2 (London, 1891).

M.Spiro, 'Religion: Problems of Definition and explanation', in Banton, *Anthropological Approaches*, 85-126.

Staveley, *Voting* E.S.Staveley, *Greek and Roman Voting and Elections* (London, 1972).

G.H.Stevenson, *Roman Provincial Administration till the Age of the Antonines* (Oxford, 1939).

A. Stewart, *Attika: Studies in Athenian Sculpture of the Hellenistic Age* (Hellenic Society Supplement 14, London, 1979).

Stockton, *Cicero* D.Stockton, *Cicero: a Political Biography* (Oxford, 1971).

Stockton, *The Gracchi* D.Stockton, *The Gracchi* (Oxford, 1979).

L.Stone, 'Prosopography', *Daedalus*, Winter 1971, 46-79.

Strong, *Roman Art* D.Strong, *Roman Art* (Harmondsworth, 1976).

Syme, *Roman Revolution* R.Syme, *The Roman Revolution* (Oxford, 1939).

G.Szemler, *The Priests of the Roman Republic* (Coll. Lat. 127, Brussels, 1972).

L.R.Taylor, 'Caesar's Colleagues in the Pontifical College', *AJPh* 63 (1942), 385-412.

Taylor, *Party Politics* L.R.Taylor, *Party Politics in the Age of Caesar* (Berkeley and Los Angeles, 1949).

L.R.Taylor, *The Voting Districts of the Roman Republic*

Rome in the Late Republic

(Papers and Monographs, American Academy in Rome, 20, Rome, 1960).

L.R.Taylor, 'Forerunners of the Gracchi', *JRS* 52 (1962), 19-27.

Taylor, *Roman Voting Assemblies*   L.R.Taylor, *Roman Voting Assemblies from the Hannibalic War to the Dictatorship of Caesar* (Ann Arbor, 1966).

L.R.Taylor and R.T.Scott, 'Seating Space in the Roman Senate and the *Senatores Pedarii*', *TAPhA* 100 (1969), 529-582.

M.Torelli, *Typology and Structure of Roman Historical Reliefs* (Ann Arbor, 1982).

G.B.Townend, 'The Poems', in T.A.Dorey (ed.), *Cicero* (London, 1965), 109-134.

A.J.Toynbee, 'Economic and Social Consequences of the Hannibalic War', *Bull.J.Ryl.Lib.* 37 (1954-55), 271-287.

A.J.Toynbee, *Hannibal's Legacy*, vol. 2 (Oxford, 1965).

J.M.C.Toynbee, *Some Notes on Artists in the Roman World* (Coll. Lat. 6, Brussels, 1951).

J.M.C.Toynbee, *Death and Burial in the Roman World* (London, 1971).

Treggiari, *Freedmen*   S.Treggiari, *Roman Freedmen in the Late Republic* (Oxford, 1969).

H.Versnel, *Triumphus* (Leiden, 1970).

Wagenvoort, *Pietas*   H.Wagenvoort, *Pietas: Selected Studies in Roman Religion* (Leiden, 1980).

F.W.Walbank, 'Polybius and Rome's Eastern Policy', *JRS* 53 (1963), 1-13.

F.W.Walbank, 'The Scipionic Legend', *PCPhS* 13 (1967), 54-69.

F.W.Walbank, *Polybius* (Berkeley, 1972).

Walker and Burnett, *Image of Augustus*   S.Walker and A. Burnett, *The Image of Augustus* (London, British Museum, 1981).

Warde-Fowler, *The Religious Experience*   W.W.Warde-Fowler, *The Religious Experience of the Roman People* (London, 1911).

J.Ward-Perkins and A. Claridge, *Pompeii AD 79* (Royal Academy of Arts Exhibition Catalogue, Bristol, 1976).

Wardman, *Rome's Debt to Greece*   A.Wardman, *Rome's Debt to Greece* (London, 1976).

Wardman, *Religion and Statecraft*   A.Wardman, *Religion and Statecraft among the Romans* (London, 1982).

A.Watson, *Law Making in the Later Roman Republic* (Oxford, 1974).

A.Watson, *Rome of the Twelve Tables*

(Princeton, 1975).

S.Weinstock, 'Two Archaic Inscriptions from Latium', *JRS* 50 (1960), 112-118.

S.Weinstock, *Divus Julius* (Oxford, 1971).

T.Wiedemann, *Greek and Roman Slavery* (London, 1981).

Williams, *Tradition and Originality*   G.Williams, *Tradition and Originality in Roman Poetry* (Oxford, 1968).

Williams, *Nature of Roman Poetry*   G.Williams, *The Nature of Roman Poetry* (Oxford, 1970)—abridged version of *Tradition and Originality*.

Williams, 'Political Patronage'   G.Williams, 'Phases in Political Patronage of Literature in Rome', in B.Gold (ed.), *Literary and Artistic Patronage in Ancient Rome* (Texas, 1982), 3-27.

A.J.N.Wilson, *Emigration from Italy in the Republican Age of Rome* (Manchester, 1966).

B.R.Wilson (ed.), *Rationality* (Oxford, 1970).

P.Winch, 'Understanding a Primitive Society', in B.R.Wilson (ed.), *Rationality* (Oxford, 1970), 78-111.

Wirszubski, *Libertas*   C.Wirszubski, *Libertas as a Political Idea at Rome during the Late Republic and Early Empire* (Cambridge, 1960).

T.P.Wiseman, 'The Ambitions of Quintus Cicero', *JRS* 56 (1966), 108-115.

T.P.Wiseman, 'The Census in the First Century BC', *JRS* 59 (1969), 59-75.

T.P.Wiseman, 'The Definition of 'Eques Romanus' in the Late Republic and Early Empire', *Historia* 19 (1970), 67-83.

Wiseman, *New Men*   T.P.Wiseman, *New Men in the Roman Senate, 139 BC—AD 14* (Oxford, 1971).

Wiseman, *Cinna the Poet*   T.P.Wiseman, *Cinna the Poet and other Roman Essays* (Leicester, 1974).

Wiseman, *Clio's Cosmetics*   T.P.Wiseman, *Clio's Cosmetics: Three Studies in Greco-Roman Literature* (Leicester, 1979).

Wiseman, 'Poets and Patrons',   T.P.Wiseman, '*Pete Nobiles Amicos*: Poets and Patrons in Late Republican Rome', in B.K.Gold (ed.), *Literary and Artistic Patronage in Ancient Rome* (Texas, 1982), 28-49.

T.P.Wiseman, '*Domi Nobiles* and the Roman Cultural Elite', in *Les 'Bourgeoisies' municipales Italiennes au IIe et Ier siècles avant J.C.* (Naples, 1983), 299-307.

M.Wistrand, *Cicero Imperator: Studies in Cicero's Correspondence 51—47 BC* (Studia Graeca et

Latina Gothoburgensia 41, Göteborg, 1979).
R.E.Witt, *Isis in the Graeco-Roman World* (London, 1971).
Z.Yavetz, 'The Living Conditions of the Urban Plebs in Republican Rome', *Latomus* 17 (1958), 500-517 (repr. in Seager, *Crisis*, 162-179).
Z.Yavetz, *Plebs and Princeps* (Oxford, 1969).
Z.Yavetz, *Julius Caesar and his Public Image* (London, 1983).

Index